Married Love; or, Love in Marriage

Marie Carmichael Stopes

Edited by Dr. William J. Robinson

MARRIED LOVE

OR

LOVE IN MARRIAGE

BY

MARIE CARMICHAEL STOPES, Sc.D., Ph.D.

DOCTOR OF SCIENCE, LONDON, DOCTOR OF PHILOSOPHY MUNICH;
FELLOW OF UNIVERSITY COLLEGE, LONDON; FELLOW OF
THE ROYAL SOCIETY OF LITERATURE, AND THE
LINNEAN SOCIETY, LONDON

With Preface and Notes, by
WILLIAM J. ROBINSON, M.D.

1918

THE CRITIC AND GUIDE COMPANY
12 MT. MORRIS PARK WEST
NEW YORK

CONTENTS

Editor's Preface

The truly monogamic couple, where the man and the woman go chaste to the marriage-bed, and go through life in mutual love and respect, these feelings growing stronger as the years go by, finding full satisfaction in each other, without any desire for any other man or woman – what nobler, what more appealing ideal can one conjure up? Nor is it an utterly unrealizable ideal, for in spite of the sneers of the cynics, there are such couples, even at the present time and even in our largest Babylons...

We cannot prevent the cynics from sneering, but even they must admit that monogamy is here, is the dominant system, is the only socially approved and legally permitted system, and we have to deal with it. And those radical sexologists who do not believe that monogamy is the best system of sexual relationship, who are sure that it will not survive for all eternity, that it will be replaced in the future by a higher adjustment, will agree, even if they do so reluctantly, that for a few years to come – say five hundred to a thousand – it will be the only feasible, the only socially admissible and legally sanctioned system.

This being the case, it becomes the sexologist's most sacred duty to do everything in his power to make the monogamic relationship as pleasant as possible, to remove as far as possible all removable causes of friction, to steer the frail matrimonial bark in safe channels, to guard it from being wrecked on the Scylla of asceticism or the Charybdis of excess; in short to help the Man and the Woman to go through life in mutual love and respect, finding full satisfaction in each other, without any desire for any other man or woman.

This is the object of Dr. Stopes' fine book. It would be too soon to expect any one work to succeed in converting every home from the hell that it often is into the paradise that it should be; but if a careful reading of it preserves the temper of some men, improves the health and cures the insomnia of some women, if it saves a few homes from disruption, it will be decidedly worth while, and its author will be called blessed – and will deserve to be.

There is plenty of love outside of marriage; there is not enough in marriage; and they who labor to augment and intensify Love in Marriage are doing good pro-social work.

Dr. William J. Robinson

Author's Preface

MORE than ever to-day are happy homes needed. It is my hope that this book may serve the State by adding to their number. Its object is to increase the joys of marriage, and to show how much sorrow may be avoided.

The only secure basis for a present-day State is the welding of its units in marriage: but there is rottenness and danger at the foundations of the State if many of the marriages are unhappy. To-day, marriage is far less happy than appears on the surface. Too many who marry expecting joy are bitterly disappointed; and the demand for "freedom" grows: while those who cry aloud are generally unaware that it is more likely to have been their own ignorance than the "marriage-bond" which was the origin of their unhappiness.

It is never easy to make marriage a lovely thing; and it is an achievement beyond the powers of the selfish, or the mentally cowardly. Knowledge is needed, and as things are at present, knowledge is almost unobtainable by those who are most in want of it.

The problems of the sex-life are infinitely complex, and for their solution urgently demand both sympathy and scientific research.

I have some things to say about sex, which, so far as I am aware, have not yet been said, or if said will bear repeating and reëmphasizing, things which seem to me to be of profound importance to men and women who hope to make their marriage beautiful.

This little book is less a record of a research than an attempt to present in easily understandable form the clarified and crystallized results of long and patient investigations. Its simple statements are based on a very large number of first hand observations, on confidences from men and women of all classes and types, and on facts gleaned from wide reading.

My original contributions to the age-long problems of marriage will be found principally in Chapter IV; also in Chapters V, and VIII. The other chapters fill in what I hope is an undistorted and unexaggerated picture of the potential beauties and realities of marriage.

The whole is written simply, and for the ordinary untrained reader, though it embodies some observations which will be new even to those who have made scientific researches on the subjects of sex and human physiology.

I do not touch upon the many human variations and abnormalities which bulk so largely in most books on sex, nor do I deal with the many problems raised by incurably unhappy marriages.

In the following pages I speak to those – and in spite of all our neurotic literature and plays, they are in the great majority – who are normal, and who are married or about to be married, and hope, but do not know how, to make their marriages happy and successful.

To the reticent, as to the conventional, it may seem a presumption or a superfluity to speak of the details of the most complex of all human functions. They ask: Is not instinct enough? The answer is: No, instinct is not enough. In every other human activity it has been realized that training is essential to creatures of intellectual capacity like ourselves. As Saleeby once wisely pointed out: A cat knows how to manage her new-born kittens, how to bring them up and teach them; a human mother does not know how to manage her baby unless she is trained, either directly or by her own quick observation. A cat performs her simple duties by instinct; a human mother has to be trained to fulfill her very complex ones.

And the same is true, and even to a greater extent, in the subtle complexities of sex. In civilized countries, in modern times, the old traditions, the profound primitive knowledge of the needs of both sexes have been lost – and nothing but a muffled confusion of individual gossip disturbs a silence, shame-faced or foul. Here and there, in a family of fine tradition, a youth or maiden may learn some of the mysteries of marriage, but the great majority of people in the English speaking countries have no glimmering of knowledge of the supreme human art, the Art of Love. And even in books on advanced Physiology and Medicine the gaps, the omissions and even the misstatements, are amazing.

In my own marriage I paid such a terrible price for sex-ignorance that I feel that knowledge gained at such a price should be placed at the service of humanity.

In this book, average, healthy, mating creatures who come within the limits of what may be called "normal," will find information which should be known to every one of our race – but is not – and which may save them years of heartache and blind groping in the dark.

The Heart's Desire

"She gave him comprehension of the meaning of love: a word in many mouths, not often explained. With her, wound in his idea of her, he perceived it to signify a new start in our existence, a finer shoot of the tree stoutly planted in good gross earth; the senses running their live sap, and the minds companioned, and the spirits made one by the whole-natured conjunction. In sooth, a happy prospect for the sons and daughters of Earth, divinely indicating more than happiness: the speeding of us, compact of what we are, between the ascetic rocks and the sensual whirlpools, to the creation of certain nobler races, now very dimly imagined."

– George Meredith, *Diana of the Crossways.*

EVERY heart desires a mate. For some reason beyond our comprehension, nature has so created us that we are incomplete in ourselves; neither man nor woman singly can know the joy in the performance of all the human functions; neither man nor woman singly can create another human being. This fact, which is expressed in our outward divergences of form, influences and colors the whole of our lives; and there is nothing for which the innermost spirit of one and all so yearns as for a sense of union with another soul, and the perfecting of oneself which such union brings.

In all young people, unless they have inherited depraved or diseased tendencies, the old desire of our race springs up afresh in its pristine beauty.

With the dreams and bodily changes of adolescence, come to the youth and maiden the strange and powerful impulses of sex. The bodily differences of the two, now accentuated, become mystical, alluring, enchanting in their promise. Their differences unite and hold together the man and the woman so that their bodily union is the solid nucleus of an immense fabric of interwoven strands reaching to the uttermost ends of the earth; some lighter than the filmiest cobweb, or than the softest wave of music, iridescent with the colors not only of the visible rainbow, but of all the invisible glories of the wave-lengths of the soul.

However much he may conceal it under assumed cynicism, worldliness, or self-seeking, the heart of every young man yearns with a great longing for the fulfilment of the beautiful dream of a life-long union with a mate. Each heart knows instinctively that it is only one's mate who can give full comprehension of all the potential greatness in one's soul, and have tender laughter for all the child-like wonder that lingers so enchantingly even in the white-haired.

The search for a mate is a quest for an understanding soul clothed in a body beautiful, but unlike our own.

In the modern world, those who set off on high endeavors or who consciously separate themselves from the ordinary course of social life, are comparatively few, and it is not to them that I am speaking. The great majority of our citizens – both men and women – after a time of waiting, or of exploring, or of oscillating from one attraction to another, "settle down" and marry.

Very few are actually so cynical as to marry without the hope of happiness; while most young people, however their words may deny it and however they may conceal their tender hopes by an assumption of cynicism, reveal that they are conscious of entering on a new and glorious state by their radiant looks and the joyous buoyancy of their actions. In the kisses and the hand-touch of the betrothed are a zest and exhilaration which stir the blood like wine. The two read poetry, listen entranced to music which echoes the songs of their pulses, and see reflected in each other's eyes the beauty of the world. In the midst of this celestial intoxication they naturally assume that, as they are on the threshold of their lives, so too they are in but the antechamber of their experience of spiritual unity.

The more sensitive, the more romantic, and the more idealistic is the young person of either sex, the more his or her soul craves for some kindred soul with whom the whole being can unite. But all have some measure of this desire, even the most prosaic, and we know from innumerable stories that the sternest man of affairs, he who may have worldly success of every sort, may yet, through the lack of a real mate, live with a sense almost as though the limbs of his soul had been amputated. Edward Carpenter has beautifully voiced this longing:

"That there should exist one other person in the world towards whom all openness of interchange should establish itself, from whom there should be no concealment; whose body should be as dear to one, in every part, as one's own; with whom there should be no sense of Mine or Thine, in property or possession; into whose mind one's thoughts should naturally flow, as it were to know themselves and to receive a new illumination; and between whom and oneself there should be a spontaneous rebound of sympathy in all the joys and sorrows and experiences of life; such is perhaps one of the dearest wishes of the soul."

– Love's Coming of Age.

It may chance that some one into whose hands this book falls may protest that he or she has never felt the fundamental yearning to form a part of that trinity which alone is the perfect expression of humanity. If that is the case, it is possible that all unconsciously he may be suffering from a real malady – sexual anesthesia. This is the name given to an inherent coldness, which, while it lacks the usual human impulse of tenderness, is generally quite unconscious of its lack. It may even be that the reader's departure from the ordinary ranks of mankind is still more fundamental, in which case, instead of sitting in judgment on the majority, he would do well to read some such books as those of Forel, Havelock Ellis, Bloch, or Krafft-Ebing, in order that his own nature may be made known to him. He may then discover to which type of our widely various humanity he belongs. He need not read my book, for it is written about, and it is written for, ordinary men and women, who feeling themselves incomplete, yearn for a union that will have power not only to make a fuller and richer thing of their own lives, but which will place them in a position to use their sacred trust as creators of lives to come.

It has happened many times in human history that individuals have not only been able to conquer this natural craving for a mate, but have set up celibacy as a higher ideal. In its most beautiful expression and sublimest manifestations, the celibate ideal has proclaimed a world-wide love, in place of the narrower human love of home and children. Many saints and sages, reformers, and dogmatists have modeled their lives on this ideal. But such individuals cannot be taken as the standard of the race, for they are out of its main current: they are branches which may flower, but never fruit in a bodily form.

In this world our spirits not only permeate matter but find their only expression through its medium. So long as we are human we must have bodies, and bodies obey chemical and physiological, as well as spiritual laws.

If our race as a whole set out to pursue an ideal which must ultimately eliminate bodies together, it is clear that very soon we should find the conditions of our environment so altered that we could no longer speak of the human race.

In the meantime, we are human. We each and all live our lives according to laws, some of which we have begun to understand, many of which are completely hidden from us. The most complete human being is he or she who consciously or unconsciously obeys the profound physical laws of our being in such a way that the spirit receives much help and as little hindrance from the body as possible. A mind or spirit finds its fullest expression thwarted by the misuse or the gross abuse of the body in which it dwells. By the ignorant or self-indulgent breaking of fundamental laws, the deepest harmonies are dislocated. The small-minded ascetic endeavors to grow spiritually by destroying his physical instincts instead of by using them.

But I would proclaim that we are set in the world so to mold matter that it may express our spirit; that it is presumption to profess to fight the immemorial laws of our physical being, and that he who does so loses unconsciously the finest flux in which wondrous new creations take their rise.

To use a homely simile – one might compare two human beings to two wires through which pass electric currents. Isolated from each other the electric forces within them pass uninterrupted along their length, but if these wires come into the right juxtaposition, the force is transmuted, and a spark, a glow of burning light arises between them. Such is love.

From the body of the loved one's simple, sweetly colored flesh, which our animal instincts urge us to desire, there springs not only the wonder of a new bodily life, but also the enlargement of the horizon of human sympathy and the glow of spiritual understanding which one could never have attained alone.

Many reading this may feel conscious that they have had physical union without such spiritual accompaniments, perhaps even without an accession of ordinary pleasure. If that is so, it can only be because, consciously or unconsciously, they have broken some of the profound laws which govern the love of man and woman. Only by learning to hold a bow correctly can one draw music from a violin. Only by obedience to the laws of the lower plane can one step up to the plane above.

The Broken Joy

"What shall be done to quiet the heart-cry of the world? How answer the dumb appeal for help we so often divine below eyes that laugh?"

—A. E. in *The Hero in Man*.

DREAMING of happiness, feeling that at last they have each found the one who will give eternal understanding and tenderness, the young man and maiden marry.

At first, in the time generally called the honeymoon, the unaccustomed freedom and the sweetness of the relation often do bring real happiness. How long does it last? Generally, a far shorter time than is generally acknowledged.

In the first joy of their union it is hidden from the two young people that they know little or nothing about the fundamental laws of each other's being. Much of the sex-attraction (not only among human beings, but even throughout the whole of the animal world) depends upon the differences between the two that pair; and probably taking them all unawares, those very differences which drew them together now begin to work their undoing. But so long as the first illusion that each understands the other is supported by the thrilling delight of ever-fresh discoveries, the sensations lived through are so rapid, and so joyous that the lovers do not realize that there is no firm foundation beneath their feet. While even in the happiest cases there may be divergences about religion, politics, social customs and opinions on things in general, these, with good will, patience, and intelligence on either side, can be ultimately adjusted, because in all such things there is a common meeting ground for the two. Human beings, while differing widely about every conceivable subject in these human relations, have at least thought about them, threshed them out, and discussed them openly for generations.

But about the much more fundamental and vital problems of sex, there is a lack of knowledge so abysmal and so universal that its mists and shadowy darkness have affected even the few who lead us, and who are prosecuting research in these subjects. And the two young people begin to suffer from fundamental divergences, before perhaps they realize that such exist, and with little prospect of ever gaining a rational explanation of them.

Nearly all those, whose own happiness seems to be dimmed or broken, count themselves exceptions, and comfort themselves with the thought of some of their friends, who they feel sure have attained the happiness which they themselves have missed.

It is generally supposed that happy people, like happy nations, have no history – they are silent about their own affairs. Those who talk about their marriage are generally those who have missed the happiness they expected. True as this may be in general, it is not permanently and profoundly true. There are people who are reckoned, and still reckon themselves, happy, but who yet, unawares, reveal the secret disappointment which clouds their inward peace.

Leaving out of account "femmes incomprises" and all the innumerable cases of neurotic, supersensitive, and slightly abnormal people, it still remains an astonishing and tragic fact that so large a proportion of normal marriages lose their early bloom and are to some extent unhappy.

For years many men and women have confided to me the secrets of their lives; and of all the innumerable cases in which the circumstances are known to me, there are tragically few marriages which approach even humanly attainable joy.

Many of those considered by the world, by the relatives, even by the loved and loving partner, to be perfectly happy marriages, are secret tragedies to the more sensitive of the pair.

Where the bride is, as are most of our educated girls, composed of virgin sweetness shut in ignorance, the man is often the first to create "the rift within the lute"; but his suffering begins almost simultaneously with hers. Unconscious of the nature, and even perhaps of the existence of his fault, he is bewildered and pained by her inarticulate pain. It is my experience, that in the early days of marriage, the young man is even more sensitive, more romantic, more easily pained about all ordinary things than the woman, that he enters marriage hoping for an even higher degree of spiritual and bodily unit than does the girl or the woman. But the man is more quickly blunted, more swiftly rendered cynical, and is readier to look upon happiness as a utopian dream than is his mate.

On the other hand, the woman is slower to realize disappointment, and more often is the more profoundly wounded by the sex-life of marriage, with a slow corrosive wound that eats into her very being.

Perfect happiness is a unity composed of a myriad essences; and this one supreme thing is exposed to the attacks of countless destructive factors.

Were I to touch upon all the possible sources of marital disappointment and unhappiness, this book would expand into a dozen bulky volumes. As I am addressing those who I assume have read, or can read, other books written upon various ramifications of the subject, I will not discuss the themes which have been handled by many writers.

In the last few years there has been such an awakening to the realization of the corrosive horror of all aspects of prostitution that there is no need to elaborate the point that no marriage can be happy where the husband has, in buying another body, sold his own health, and is tainted with disease.

Nor is it necessary, in speaking to well-meaning, optimistic young couples, to enlarge upon the obvious dangers of drunkenness, self-indulgence, and the cruder forms of selfishness. It is with the subtler infringements of the fundamental laws we have to deal. And the prime tragedy is that, as a rule, the two young people are both unaware of the existence of such decrees. Yet here, as elsewhere in nature, the lawbreaker is punished whether he is aware of the existence of the law he breaks or not.

In the state of ignorance which so largely predominates to-day, the first sign that things are amiss between the two who thought they were entering paradise together, is generally a sense of loneliness, a feeling that the one who was expected to have all in common, is outside some experience, some subtle delight, and fails to understand the needs of the loved one. Trivialities are often the first indicators of something which takes its roots unseen in the profoundest depths of our natures. The girl may sob for hours over something that at first appears so trifling that she cannot even tell a friend about it, while the young man, who thought that he had set out with his soul's beloved upon an adventure into celestial distances, may find himself apparently up against some barrier in her which appears incomprehensible or frivolous.

Then, so strange is the mystical inter-relation between our bodies, our minds, and our souls, that for crimes committed in ignorance of the dual functions of the married pair, and the laws which harmonize them, the punishments are reaped on plains quite diverse, till new and ever new misunderstandings appear to spring spontaneously from the soil of their mutual contact. Gradually or swiftly each heart begins to hide a sense of boundless isolation. It may be urged that this statement is too sweeping. It is, however, based on innumerable actual cases. I have heard from women, whose marriages are looked upon by all as the happiest possible expressions of human felicity, the details of secret pain of which they have allowed their husbands no inkling. Many men will know how they have hidden from their beloved wives a sense of dull disappointment, perhaps at her coldness in the marital embrace, or from the feeling that there is in her something elusive which always evades their grasp.

Now that so many "movements" are abroad, folk on all sides are emboldened to express the opinion that it is marriage itself which is at fault. Many think that merely by loosening the bonds, and making it possible to start afresh with some one else, their lives would be made harmonious and happy. By many such reformers it is forgotten that he or she who knows nothing of the way to make marriage great and beautiful with one partner, is not likely to succeed with another. Only by a reverent study of the Art of Love can the beauty of its expression be realized in linked lives.

And even when once learnt, the Art of Love takes time to practice. As Ellen Key says, "Love requires peace, love will dream; it cannot live upon the remnants of our time and our personality."

There is no doubt that Love loses, in the haste and bustle of our modern turmoil, not only much of its charm and grace, but some of its vital essence. The result of the haste which so infests and poisons us, is often felt much more by the woman than by the man. The over-stimulation of city life tends to "speed up" the man's reactions, but to retard hers. To make matters worse, even for those who have leisure to spend on love-making, the opportunities for peaceful, romantic dalliance are less to-day in a city with its tubes and cinema shows than in woods and gardens where the pulling of rosemary or lavender may be the sweet excuse for the slow and profound mutual rousing of passion. Now, physical passion, so swiftly stimulated in man, tends to override all else, and the untutored male sees but one thing – the accomplishment of desire. The woman, for it is in her nature so to do, forgives the crudeness, but sooner or later her love revolts, probably in secret, and then forever after, though she may command an outward tenderness, she has nothing within but scorn and loathing for the act which should have been a perpetually recurring entrancement.

So many people are now born and bred in artificial and false surroundings, that even the elementary fact that the acts of love should be joyous is unknown to them. Havelock Ellis ("Psychology of Sex," vol. 6, 1913, p. 512) quotes the amazing statement of a distinguished American gynecologist, who said, "I do not believe mutual pleasure in the sexual act has any particular bearing on the happiness of life." This is, perhaps, an extreme case, yet so many distinguished medical men, gynecologists and physiologists, are either in ignorance or error regarding some of the profoundest facts of human sex-life, that it is not surprising that ordinary young couples, however hopeful, should break and destroy the joy that might have been their lifelong companion.

Woman's "Contrariness"

"Oh! for that Being whom I can conceive to be in the world, though I shall not live to prove it. One to whom I might have recourse in all my Humors and Dispositions: in all my Distempers of Mind, visionary Causes of Mortification, and Fairy Dreams of Pleasure. I have been trying to train up a Lady or two for these good offices of Friendship, but hitherto I must not boast of my success."

– Herrick.

WHAT is the fate of the average man who marries, happily and hopefully, a girl well suited to him? He desires with his whole heart a mutual, lifelong happiness. He marries with the intention of fulfilling every injunction given him by father, doctor, and friend. He is considerate in trifles, he speaks no harsh words, he and his bride go about together, walk together, read together, and perhaps, if they are very advanced, even work together. But after a few months, or maybe a few years, of marriage they seem to have drifted apart, and he finds her often cold and incomprehensible. If he is a nice man, he will not acknowledge this even to his best friend. But his heart knows its own pain.

He may at times laugh, and in the friendliest spirit tease her about her contrariness. That is taken by every one to mean nothing but a playful concealment of his profound love. Probably it is. But gnawing at the very roots of his love is a hateful little worm – the sense that she is contrary. He feels that she is at times inexplicably cold; that, sometimes, when he has "done nothing" she will have tears in her eyes, irrational tears which she cannot explain.

He observes that one week his tender love-making and romantic advances win her to smiles and joyous yielding, and then perhaps a few days later the same, or more impassioned, tenderness on his part is met by coldness or a forced appearance of warmth, which, while he may make no comment upon it, hurts him acutely. And this deep, inexplicable hurt is often the beginning of the end of love. Men like to feel that they understand their beloved, and that she is a rational being.

After this has continued for some time, if the man is of at all a jealous nature he will search among his wife's acquaintances for some one whom she may have met, for some one who may momentarily have diverted her attention. For the natural man at once seeks the explanation of his own ill-success in a rival. On some occasion when her coldness puzzles him he is conscious that his love, his own desires, are as ardent as they were a few days before. Knowing so intimately his own heart, he is sure of the steadiness of its love, and he feels acutely the romantic passion to which her beauty stirs him. He remembers perhaps that a few days earlier his ardor had awakened a response in her. Therefore he reaches what appears to him to be the infallible logical deduction: that either there must be some rival – or his bride's nature is incomprehensible, contrary, capricious. Both – thoughts to madden.

With capriciousness, man in general has little patience. Caprice renders his best efforts null and void. Woman's caprice is, or appears to be, a negation of reason. And as reason is man's most precious and hard-won faculty, the one which has raised mankind from the ranks of brute creation, he cannot bear to see it apparently flouted.

That his bride should lack logic and sweet reasonableness – is a flaw it hurts him to recognize in her. He has to crush the thought down.

It may then happen that the young man, himself pained and bewildered at having pained his bride by the very ardor of his affection, may strive to please her by placing restraint upon himself. He may ask himself: Do not books on sex preach restraint to the man? He reads the books written for the guidance of youth, and finds "restraint," "self-control," generally, and often irrationally, urged in them all. His next step may then then be to curtail the expression of his tender feelings, and to work hard and late in the evenings instead of kissing his bride's fingers and playing with the lace of her dress.

And then, if he is at all observant, he may be aggrieved and astonished to find her again wistful or hurt. With the tender longing to understand, which is so profound a characteristic in all the best of our young men, he begs, implores, or pets her into telling him some part of the reason for her fresh grievance. He discovers to his amazement that this time she is hurt because he had not made those very advances which so recently had repelled her, and had been with such difficulty repressed by his intellectual efforts.

He asks himself in despair: What is a man to do? If he is intelligent, he probably devours all the books on sex he can obtain. But in them he is not likely to find much real guidance. He learns from them that "restraint" is advised by practically every author, but according to the character of the author he will find that "restraint" means having the marriage relation with his wife not more than three times a week, or once a month – or never at all except for the protection of children. He finds no rational guidance based on natural law.

According to his temperament then, he may begin to practice "restraint."

But it may happen, and indeed it has probably happened in every marriage once or many times, that the night comes when the man who has heroically practiced restraint, accidentally discovers his wife's tears on her solitary pillow.

He seeks for advice indirectly from his friends, perhaps from his doctor. But can his local doctor or his friends tell him more than the chief European authorities on this subject? In Forel's "The Sexual Question," he reads the following advice: *The reformer, Luther, who was a practical man, laid down the average rule of two or three connections a week in marriage, at the time of highest sexual power. I may say that my numerous observations as a physician have generally confirmed this rule, which seems to me to conform very well to the normal state to which man*[1] *has become gradually adapted during thousands of years. Husbands who would consider this average as an imprescriptible right would, however, make wrong pretensions, for it is quite possible for a normal man to contain himself much longer, and it is his duty to do so, not only when his wife is ill, but also during menstruation and pregnancy."*

Many men will not be so considerate as to follow this advice, which represents a high standard of living; but, on the other hand, there are many who are willing to go not only so far, but further than this in their self-suppression in order to attain their heart's desire, the happiness of their mate, and consequently their own life's joy.

However willing they may be to go further, the great question for the man is: How far?

There are innumerable leaders anxious to lead in many different directions. The young husband may try first one and then the other, and still find his wife unsatisfied, incomprehensible – capricious. Then it may be that, disheartened, he gets tired and she sinks into the dull apathy of acquiescence in her "wifely duty." He is left with an echo of resentment in his heart; if only she had not been so capricious, they would still have been happy, he fancies.

Many writers, novelists, poets and dramatists have represented the uttermost tragedy of human life as due to the incomprehensible contrariness of the feminine nature. The kindly ones smile, perhaps a little patronizingly, and tell us that women are more instinctive, more child-like, less reasonable than men. The bitter ones sneer or reproach or laugh at this "contrariness" in women they do not understand, and which, baffling their intellect, appears to them to be irrational folly.

It seems strange that those who search for natural law in every domain of the universe should have so neglected the most vital subject, the one which concerns us all infinitely more than the naming of planets or the collecting of insects. Woman is not essentially capricious. Some of the laws of her being might have been discovered long ago had the existence of law been suspected. But it has been easier, has suited the general structure of society much better, for men to shrug their shoulders and smile at women as irrational and capricious creatures.

Vaguely, perhaps, men have realized that much of the charm of life lies in the sex-differences between men and women; so they have snatched at the easy theory that women differ from themselves by being capricious. Moreover, by attributing to mere caprice the coldness which at times comes over the most ardent woman, man was unconsciously justifying himself by coercing her to suit himself.

Conditions have been such that hitherto the explorers and scientific investigators, the historians and statisticians, the poets and artists have been mainly men. Consequently woman's side of the sexual life has found little or no expression. Woman has been content to mold herself to the shape desired by man wherever possible, and she has stifled her natural feelings and her own deep thoughts as they welled up.

Most women have never realized intellectually, but many have been dimly half-conscious, that woman's nature is set to rhythms over which man has almost no more control than he has over the tides of the sea. While the ocean can subdue and dominate man and laugh at his attempted restrictions, woman has bowed to man's desire over her body, and, regardless of its pulses, he approaches her or not as is his will. Some of her rhythms defy him – the moon-month tide of menstruation, the cycle of ten moon-months of bearing the growing child and its birth at the end of the tenth wave – these are essentials too strong to be mastered by man. But the subtler ebb and flow of woman's sex has escaped man's observation or his care.

If a swimmer comes to a sandy beach when the tide is out and the waves have receded, leaving sand where he had expected deep blue water – does he, balked of his bath, angrily call the sea "capricious"?

But the tenderest bridegroom finds only caprice in his bride's coldness when she yields her sacrificial body while her sex-tide is at the ebb.

There is another side to this problem, one perhaps even less considered by society. There is the case of the loving woman whose love-tide is at the highest, and whose husband does not recognize the signs of her ardor. In our anæmic artificial days it often happens that the man's desire is a surface need, quickly satisfied, colorless, and lacking beauty, and that he has no knowledge of the rich complexities of love-making which an initiate of love's mysteries enjoys. To such a man his wife may indeed seem petulant, capricious, or resentful without reason.

Welling up in her are the wonderful tides, scented and enriched by the myriad experiences of the human race from its ancient days of leisure and flower-wreathed love-making, urging her to transports and to self-expressions, were the man but ready to take the first step in the initiative, or to recognize and welcome it in her. Seldom dare any woman, still more seldom dare a wife, risk the blow at her heart which would be given were she to offer charming love-play to which the man did not respond. To the initiate she will be able to reveal that the tide is up by a hundred subtle signs, upon which he will seize with delight. But if her husband is blind to them there is for her nothing but silence, self-suppression, and their inevitable sequence of self-scorn, followed by resentment towards the man who places her in such a position while talking of his "love."

So little of the elements of the Art of Love do many men know that the case of Mrs. G. is not exceptional. Her husband was accustomed to pet her and to have relations with her frequently, but yet he never took any trouble to rouse her sex-feelings. She had married as a very innocent girl, but often vaguely felt a sense of something lacking in her husband's love. Her husband had never kissed her except on the lips or cheeks, but once at the crest of the wave of her sex-tide (all unconscious that it was so) she felt a yearning to feel his head, his lips, pressed against her bosom. The sensitive interrelation between a woman's breasts and the rest of her sex-life is a well-established fact, and there is a world of poetic beauty in the longing of a loving woman for the unconceived child, which melts in mists of tenderness toward her lover, the soft touch of whose lips can thus rouse her mingled joy. Because she shyly asked him, Mrs. G.'s husband impressed one short kiss on her bosom, and never repeated it. He was so ignorant that he did not know that the kissing and the tender fondling with his lips of a woman's breasts is one of the first and surest ways to make her ready for complete and satisfactory union. In this way he inhibited her natural desire, and as he never did anything to stir it, she never had any physical pleasure in their relation. Such prudish or careless husbands, content with their own satisfaction, little know the pent-up aching, or even resentment, which may eat into their wife's joy.

In many cases, however, the man is also the victim of the social customs which make sex-knowledge for women taboo.

It has become a tradition of our social life that the ignorance of woman about her own body and that of her future husband is a flower-like innocence. And to such an extreme is this sometimes pushed, that not seldom is a girl married unaware that married life will bring her into physical relations with her husband, fundamentally different from those with her brother.[2] When she discovers the true nature of his body, and learns the part she has to play as a wife, she may refuse utterly to agree to her husband's wishes. I know a case in which the husband, chivalrous and loving, had to wait years before his bride recovered from the shock of the discovery of the meaning of marriage and was able to allow him a natural relation. There are known not a few cases in which the horror of the first night of marriage with a man less considerate, has driven the bride to suicide or insanity.

That girls can reach a marriageable age without some knowledge of the realities of sex would seem incredible: but it is a fact. One highly educated lady whom I know intimately told me that when she was about eighteen she suffered many months of agonizing apprehension that she was about to have a baby, because a man had snatched a kiss from her lips at a dance.

When girls so brought up are married it is rape for the husband to insist on his "marital rights" at once. It will be difficult or impossible for such a bride ever after to experience the joys of sex-union, for such a beginning must imprint upon her consciousness the view that the man's animal nature dominates him.

In a magazine I came across a poem which vividly expresses this peculiarly feminine sorrow:

" . . . To mate with men who have no soul about
    Earth grubbing; who, the bridal night, forsooth,
Killed sparks that rise from instinct fires of life,
    And left us frozen things, alone to fashion
Our souls to dust, masked with the name of wife –
    Long years of youth – love years – the years of passion
Yawning before us. So, shamming to the end,
    All shriveled by the side of him we wed,
Hoping that peace may riper years attend,
    Mere odalisques are we – well housed, well fed."

    -Katherine Nelson.

Many men who enter marriage sincerely and tenderly, may yet have some previous experience of bought "love." It is then not unlikely that they may fall into the error of explaining their wife's experiences in terms of the reactions of the prostitute. They argue that, because the prostitute showed physical excitement and pleasure in the sexual act, if the bride or wife does not do so, then she is "cold" or "undersexed." They may not realize that often all the bodily movements of the prostitute are studied and simulated because her client enjoys his orgasm best when he imagines that the woman in his arms has one simultaneously.

As Forel says: "The company of prostitutes often renders men incapable of understanding feminine psychology, for prostitutes are hardly more than automata trained for the use of male sensuality. When men look among these for the sexual psychology of woman they find only their own mirror."

Fate is often cruel to men, too. It may be that after years of fighting with his hot young blood a man has given up, and gone now and then for relief to prostitutes, and then later in life has met the woman who is his mate, and whom, after remorse for his soiled past, he marries. Then, unwittingly, he may make the wife suffer either by interpreting her in the light of the other women, or perhaps (though this happens less frequently) by setting her absolutely apart from them. I know of a man who, after a loose life, met a woman whom he reverenced and adored. He married her, but to preserve her "purity," her difference from the others, he never had sexual relations with her.[3] She was strangely unhappy, for she loved him passionately and longed for children. She appeared to him to be pining "capriciously" when she became thin and neurotic.

Perhaps if this man had known that some female animals suffer severely and may even die if denied sexual union,[4] he might have seen his own behaviour in a truer light.

The idea that woman is lowered or "soiled" by sexual intercourse is still deeply rooted in some strata of our society. Many sources have contributed to this mistaken idea, not the least powerful being the ascetic ideal of the early church, and the fact that man has used woman as his instrument so often regardless of her wishes. Women's education and the trend of social feeling have largely been in the direction of encouraging the idea that sex-life is a low, physical, and degrading necessity which a pure woman is above enjoying.

In marriage the husband has used his "marital right"[5] of intercourse when he wished it. Both law and custom have strengthened the view that he has the right to approach his wife whenever he wishes, and that she has no wishes and no fundamental needs in the matter at all.

That woman has a rhythmic sex-tide which if its seasons were obeyed would ensure not only her enjoyment, but would explode the myth of her capriciousness, seems not to be suspected. We have studied the wave-lengths of water, of sound, of light; but when will the sons and daughters of men study the sex-tide in woman and learn the laws of her Periodicity of Recurrence of Desire?

Footnotes

1. The italics are mine. – M. C. S. This pronouncement of an exceptionally advanced and broad-minded thinker serves to show

how little attention has hitherto been paid to the woman's side of this question, or to ascertaining her natural requirements.

2. To our blasé men and women about town, this statement may appear ridiculous, fantastic or exaggerated. But it represents a true state of affairs. Girls who get married in complete ignorance of what the marriage relation implies still exist to-day, in the year 1918. – W. J. R.

3. Such cases while rare are not altogether mythical, but the cause is generally to be found elsewhere. In some cases the abstinence is due to nothing more nor less than acquired impotence, the man's inability to perform the act. In other cases the reason may be found in a previous venereal disease and the man's consequent fear to infect his wife. Consciously or unconsciously the man makes a virtue out of necessity.

4. See Marshall, Quarterly Journal Microscopic Science, Vol. 48, 1904, p. 323.

5. "Conjugal Rights," Notes and Queries, May 16, 1891, p. 383. "S. writes from the Probate Registry, Somerset House: 'Previous to 1733 legal proceedings were recorded in Latin, and the word then used where we now speak of rights was obsequies. For some time after the substitution of English for Latin the term rites was usually, if not invariably adopted; rights would appear to be a comparatively modern error.'"

The Fundamental Pulse

"The judgments of men concerning women are very rarely matters of cold scientific observation, but are colored both by their own sexual emotions and by their own moral attitude toward the sexual impulse. . . . [Men's] Statements about the sexual impulses of woman often tell us less about women than about the persons who make them."

– H. Ellis.

BY the majority of "nice" people woman is supposed to have no spontaneous sex impulses. By this I do not mean a sentimental "falling in love," but a physical, a physiological state of stimulation which arises spontaneously and quite apart from any particular man. It is in truth the creative impulse, and is an expression of a high power of vitality. So widespread in Anglo-Saxon countries is the view that it is only depraved women who have such feelings (especially before marriage) that most women would rather die than acknowledge that they do at times feel a physical yearning indescribable, but as profound as hunger for food. Yet many, many women have shown me the truth of their natures when I have simply and naturally assumed that of course they felt it – being normal women – and have asked them only: When? From their replies I have collected facts which are sufficient to overturn many ready-made theories about women.

Some of the ridiculous absurdities which go by the name of science may be illustrated by the statement made by Windscheid in the Centralblatt für Gynäkologie: "In the normal woman, especially of the higher social classes, the sexual instinct is acquired, not inborn; when it is inborn, or awakens by itself, there is abnormality. Since women do not know this instinct before marriage, they do not miss it when they have no occasion in life to learn it."

The negation of this view is expressed in the fable of Hera quoted by Ellen Key. Hera sent Iris to earth to seek out three virtuous and perfectly chaste maidens who were unsoiled by any dreams of love.

Iris found them, but could not take them back to Olympus, for they had already been sent for to replace the superannuated Furies in the infernal regions.

Nevertheless it is true that the whole education of girls, which so largely consists in the concealment of the essential facts of life from them; and the positive teaching so prevalent that the racial instincts are low and shameful; and also the social condition which places so many women in the position of depending on their husband's will not only for the luxuries but for the necessities of life, have all tended to inhibit natural sex-impulses in women, and to conceal and distort what remains.

It is also true that in our northern climate women are on the whole naturally less persistently stirred than southerners; and it is further true that with the delaying of maturity, due to our ever-lengthening youth, it often happens that a woman is approaching or even past thirty before she is awake to the existence in her of the sex-urge. For many years before that, however, the unrealized influence, diffused throughout her very system, has profoundly affected her. It is also true that (partly due to the inhibiting influences of our customs, traditions and social code) women may marry before it wakes, and may remain long after marriage entirely unconscious that it exists subdued within them. For innumerable women, too, the husband's regular habits of intercourse, claiming her both when she would naturally enjoy union and when it is to some degree repugnant to her, have tended to flatten out the billowing curves of the line of her natural desire. One result, apparently little suspected, of using the woman as a passive instrument for man's need has been, in effect, to make her that and nothing more. Those men – and there are many – who complain of the lack of ardor in good wives, are often themselves entirely to blame for it. When a woman is claimed at times when she takes no natural pleasure in union, it reduces her vitality, and tends to kill her power of enjoying it when the love season returns.

It is certainly true of women as they have been made by the inhibitions of modern civilization, that most of them are only fully awake to the existence of sex after marriage. As we are civilized human beings, the social, intellectual, spiritual side of the love-choice have tended to mask the basic physiological aspect of women's sex-life. To find a woman in whom the currents are not all so entangled that the whole is inseparable into factors, is not easy, but I have found that wives (particularly happy wives whose feelings are not complicated by the stimulus of another love) who have been separated from their husbands for some months through professional or business duties – whose husbands, for instance, are abroad – are the women from whom the best and most definitive evidence of a fundamental rhythm of feeling can be obtained. Such women, yearning daily for the tender comradeship and nearness of their husbands, find in addition, at particular times, an accession of longing for the close physical union of the final sex-act. Many such separated wives feel this; and those I have asked to keep notes of the dates, have, with remarkable unanimity, told me that these times came specially just before and a week or so after the close of menstruation, coming, that is, about every fortnight. It is from such women that I got the first clew to the knowledge of what I call the law of Periodicity of Recurrence of desire in women.

This law it is possible to represent graphically as a curved line; a succession of crests and hollows as in all wave-lines. Its simplest and most fundamental expression, however, is generally immensely complicated by other stimulations which may bring into it diverse series of waves, or irregular wave-crests. We have all, at some time, watched the regular ripples of the sea breaking against a sand-bank, and noticed that the influx of another current of water may send a second system of waves at right angles to the first, cutting athwart them, so that the two series of waves pass through each other.

Woman is so sensitive and responsive an instrument, and so liable in our modern civilized world to be influenced by innumerable sets of stimuli, that it is perhaps scarcely surprising that the deep, underlying waves of her primitive sex-tides have been obscured and entangled so that their regular sequence has been masked in the choppy turmoil of her sea, and their existence has been largely unsuspected, and apparently quite unstudied.

For some years I have been making as scientific and detailed as study as possible of this extremely complex problem. Owing to the frank and scientific attitude of a number of women, and the ready and intimate confidence of many more, I have obtained a number of most interesting facts from which I think it is already possible to deduce a generalization which is illuminating, and may be of great medical and sociological value.

It is first necessary to consider several other features of woman's life, however.

The obvious moon-month rhythm in woman, so obvious that it cannot be overlooked, has been partially studied in its relation to some of the ordinary functions of her life. Experiments have been made to show its influence on the rate of breathing, the muscular strength, the temperature, the keenness of sight, etc., and these results have even been brought together and pictured in a single curved diagram supposed to show the variability in woman's capacities at the different times in her twenty-eight-day cycle.

But it brings home to one how little original work even in this field has yet been done, that the same identical diagram is repeated from book to book, and in Marshall's "Physiology" it is "taken from Sellheim," in Havelock Ellis "from Von Ott," and in other books is re-copied and attributed to still other sources.

This diagram appears to be the only one of its kind, and is reproduced by one learned authority after another, yet nearly every point on which this curve is based appears to have been disputed.

According to this curve, woman's vitality rises during the few days before menstruation, sinks to its lowest ebb during menstruation and rises shortly after, and then runs nearly level till it begins to rise again before the next menstrual period. This simple curve may or may not be true for woman's temperature, muscular strength, and the other relatively simple things which have been investigated. My work and observations on a large number of women all go to show that this curve does not represent the waves of woman's sex-tides.

24

The whole subject is so complex and so little studied that it is difficult to enter upon it at all without going into many details which may seem remote or dull to the general reader. Even a question which we must all have asked, and over which we have probably pondered in vain, namely: What is menstruation? cannot yet be answered. To the lay mind it would seem that this question should be answerable at once by any doctor; but many medical men are still far from being able to reply to it even approximately correctly.

There are a good many slight variations among us, ranging from a three to a five week "month," but the majority of the women of our race have a moon-month of twenty-eight days, once during which comes the flow of menstruation. If we draw out a chart with succeeding periods of 28 days each, looking on each period as a unit: When in this period is it that a normal healthy woman feels desire or any up-welling of her sex-tides?

The few statements which are made in general medical and physiological literature on the subject of sex feeling in women are generally very guarded and vague. Marshall ("Physiology of Reproduction," p. 138), for instance, says: "The period of most acute sexual feeling is generally just after the close of the menstrual period." Ellis speaks of desire being stronger before and sometimes also after menstruation, and appears to lean to the view that it is natural for desire to coincide with the menstrual flow.

After the most careful inquiries I have come to the conclusion that the general confusion regarding this subject is due partly to the great amount of variation which exists between different individuals, and partly to the fact that very few women have any idea of taking any scientific interest in life, and partly to the fact that the more profound, fundamental rhythm of sex desire which I have come to the conclusion exists or is potential in every normal woman, is covered over or masked by the more superficial and temporary influences due to a great variety of stimuli or inhibitions in modern life. For the present consideration I have tried to disentangle the profound and natural rhythm from the more irregular surface waves.

Chart No. I may assist in making graphically clear what has been said in these last few pages. It is compounded from a number of individual records, and shows a fair average chart of the rhythmic sequence of superabundance and flagging in woman's sex-vitality. The tops of the wave-crests come with remarkable regularity so that there are two wave-crests in each twenty-eight day month. The one comes on the two or three days just before menstruation: the other after; but after menstruation has ceased there is a nearly level interval, bringing the next wave-crest to the two or three days which come about eight or nine days after the close of menstruation, that is, just round the fourteen days, or half the moon month, since the last wave-crest. If this is put in its simplest way, one may say that there are fortnightly periods of desire, arranged so that one period comes always just before each menstrual flow. Upon her vitality at the time, and the general health of the woman, the length of each desire-period, or, as we might say, the size and complexity of each wave-crest, depends. Sometimes for the whole of as many as, or even more than, three days she may be ardently and quite naturally stimulated, while at another time the same woman, if she is tired or overworked, may be conscious of desire for only a few hours, or even less.

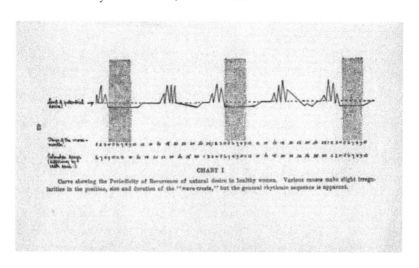

CHART I

Curve showing the Periodicity of Recurrence of natural desire in healthy women. Various causes make slight irregularities in the position, size and duration of the "wave-crests," but the general rhythmic sequence is apparent.

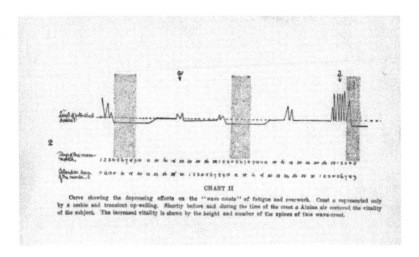

CHART II

Curve showing the depressing effects on the "wave crests" of fatigue and overwork. Crest o represented only by a feeble and transient up-welling. Shortly before and during the time of the crest a Alpine air restored the vitality of the subject. The increased vitality is shown by the height and number of the apices of this wave-crest.

The effects of fatigue, city-life, bad feeding and indeed of most outward circumstances may be very marked, and may for years, or all her life, so reduce her vitality that a woman may never have experienced any spontaneous sex-impulse at all.

The effects of fatigue, which reduces the vital energy, even in a normal, strongly sexed woman, can be seen on chart II, where at a the intermediate wave-crest is very much reduced. This is not a generalized chart, but a detailed record of an actual individual case.

Curves similar to those shown on charts I and II represent in general terms a simplified view of what my research leads me to believe to be the normal, spontaneous sex-tide in women of our race. As one young married woman confided to me, her longing for bodily union with her husband, as distinct from her longing for his daily companionship, seemed to well up naturally "like clock-work," and this when he had been long away from her. But human beings vary remarkably in every particular, and just as no two people have the same features, so no two people would have absolutely identical curves were they recorded in sufficient detail. Many a woman is particularly conscious of only one period in each moon-month. Of such women, some feel the period which comes before menstruation, and some feel the one which follows it. In those who generally feel only one, the second period is sometimes felt when they are particularly well, or only when they read exciting novels, or meet the man they love at a time coinciding with the natural but suppressed time of desire. There are a few women, who seem to be really a little abnormal, who feel the strongest desire actually during the menstrual flow.

If any one who reads this thinks to test my view by questioning a number of women, the result will probably appear very conflicting, partly because it is not often that women will tell the truth about such a thing, and partly because in the larger number of women either one or the other period is the more acute and is the one they observe in themselves – if they have observed anything. But a delicate and more accurate investigation of such cases will often bring to light the existence of the second crest of sex desire. Once the fundamental idea is grasped, much that appeared obscure or of no significance becomes plain and full of meaning. One lady doctor with whom I discussed my view at once said that it illuminated many observations she had made on her patients, but had not brought together or explained.

There is but little evidence to be found in scientific works on sex, but an interesting instance is mentioned by Forel, "The Sexual Question," in another connection. He says: "A married woman confessed to me, when I reproached her for being unfaithful to her husband, that she desired coitus at least once a fortnight, and that when her husband was not there she took the first comer." We may perhaps all see in her want of self-control a grievous moral delinquency, but in her fortnightly periods of desire she fits perfectly into the law which, it appears to me, governs the normal sex-tides of the female of our species.

In this connection it is of interest to note the decrees of the Mosaic Law regarding marital intercourse. Not only was all intercourse with a woman during her menstruation period very heavily punished (see Leviticus XX. 18: "If a man lie with a woman having her sickness...both of them shall be cut off from among their people"), but the Mosaic Law provided that women should be protected from intercourse for some days after each such period. The results obtained by my independent investigation thus find some support in this ancient wisdom of the East. Modern writers are inclined to deride the Mosaic Law on the ground that it prohibits intercourse just at the time when they think sex-feeling should be strongest. But it does not appear on what grounds they make the latter statement, nor do they give any scientific data in support of it. Thus Galabin in his "Manual of Midwifery" says: "In the Jewish law women are directed to abstain[1] from coitus during menstruation and for seven days after its cessation. Strict observers of the law are said to go beyond what is commanded in Leviticus, and even if the discharge lasts only for an hour or two, to observe five days during which the discharge might last, for the period itself, and add to these seven clear days, making twelve in all. . . . It is much to be doubted whether . . . a whole nation was ever induced to practice abstinence at the period of most acute sexual feeling." But, as will readily be recognized, the old Jewish plan of having twelve clear days after the beginning of menstruation before the next union, is in almost exact harmony with the Law of Periodicity of Recurrence of desire in woman as shown in my charts.

These comparatively simple curves represent what I would postulate as the normal spontaneous up-welling of natural desire in woman. These are the foundations on which the edifice of the physical expression of love may be built. It must not be forgotten, however, that, particularly in modern luxurious life, there are innumerable excitements which may stimulate sexual feeling, just as there are many factors in our life which tend to inhibit or retard it. A woman may be, like a man, so swayed by a great love that there is not a day in the whole month when her lover's touch, his voice, the memory of his smile, does not stir her into the thrilling longing for the uttermost union. Hence it is often difficult, particularly for a woman dwelling with the man she loves, to recognize this rhythm in herself, for she may be perpetually stimulated by her love and by his being. I am convinced, however, that ordinarily, whether she recognizes it by outward signs or not, it profoundly influences the average woman, and hence that it fundamentally affects the marriage relation in every way. The burning magnificence of an overpowering lifelong love is not given to many, and a husband who desires lasting and mutual happiness in his marriage, will carefully study his wife, observe how far she has a normal rhythm, and in what respects she possesses peculiar personal traits. He will then endeavor to adapt his demands on her so that they are in harmony with her nature.

This mutual adaptation is not an entirely simple matter, and will be considered in the next chapter.

Footnotes

1. (In Leviticus XV, it is the man who is directed to abstain from touching the woman at this period, and who is rendered unclean if he does.)

Mutual Adjustment

"Love worketh no ill to his neighbour."

–St. Paul

IN the average man of our race desire knows no seasons beyond the slight slackening of the winter months and the heightening of spring. Some men have observed in themselves a faintly-marked monthly rhythm, but in the majority of men desire, even if held in stern check, is merely slumbering. It is always present, ever ready to wake at the lightest call, and often so spontaneously insistent as to require perpetual conscious repression.

It would go ill with the men of our race had women retained the wild animals' infrequent seasonal rhythm, and with it her inviolable rights in her own body save at the mating season. Woman, too, has acquired a much more frequent rhythm; but, as it does not equal man's, he has tended to ignore and override it, coercing her at all times and seasons, either by force, or by the even more compelling power of "divine" authority and social tradition.

If man's desire is perpetual and woman's intermittent; if man's desire naturally wells up every day or every few days, and woman's only every fortnight or every month, it may appear at first sight impossible for the unwarped needs of both natures to be mutually satisfied.

The sense that a satisfactory mutual adjustment is not within the realms of possibility has, indeed, obsessed our race for centuries. The result has been that the supposed need of one of the partners has tended to become paramount, and we have established the social traditions of a husband's "rights" and wifely "duty." As one man quite frankly said to me: "As things are it is impossible for both sexes to get what they want. One must be sacrificed. And it is better for society that it should be the woman."

Nevertheless, the men who consciously sacrifice the women are in a minority. Most men act in ignorance. Our code, however, has blindly sacrificed not only the woman, but with her the happiness of the majority of men, who, in total ignorance of its meaning and results, have grown up thinking that women should submit to regularly frequent, or even nightly, intercourse. For the sake of a few moments of physical pleasure they lose realms of ever-expanding joy and tenderness; and while men and women may not realize the existence of an untrodden paradise, they both suffer, if only half consciously, from being shut out from it.

Before making some suggestions which may help married people to find not only a via media of mutual endurance, but a via perfecta of mutual joy, it is necessary to consider a few points about the actual nature of man's "desire." In the innumerable books addressed to the young which I have read, I have not found one which gives certain points regarding the meaning of the male sex-phenomena which must be grasped before it is possible to give rational guidance to intelligent young men.

The general physiology of our body is given to us in youth and in a clean scientific way. But the physiology of our most profoundly disturbing functions is ignored – in my opinion, criminally ignored.

Every mating man and woman should know at least the essential facts:

The sex-organs of a man consist not only of the testicles which give rise to the living, moving, ciliated cells, the spermatozoa, and of the channel or tube in the center of the penis through which they pass and by means of which they are directed into the proper place for their deposition, the woman's vagina. Associated with these primary and essential structures there are other tissues and glands which play subsidiary but yet very important parts. Man's penis, when quiet and unstimulated, is soft, small and drooping. But when stimulated, either by physical touch which acts through the nerves and muscles directly, or by the sight or nearness, or thought of some one lovely and beloved, which acts indirectly through messages

32

from the brain, it increases greatly in size, and becomes stiff, turgid and erect. Many men imagine that the turgid condition of an erection is due to the local accumulation of semen, and that these can only be naturally got rid of by an ejaculation. This is entirely wrong. The enlargement of the penis is not at all due to the presence of actual semen, but is due to the effects of the nervous reaction on the blood vessels, leading to the filling, principally, of the veins, and of the arteries. As the blood enters but does not leave the penis, the venous cavities in it fill up with venous blood until the whole is rigid. When rigid this organ is able to penetrate the female entrance, and there the further stimulation calls out the semen from their storehouses, the seminal vesicles, the testes and the prostate, and they pass down the channel within the penis (the urethra) and are expelled.

If this is clear, it will be realized that the stiffening and erection does not necessarily call for relief in the ejaculation of semen. If the veins can empty themselves, as they naturally do when the nervous excitement which constricted them locally passes, the erection will subside without any loss of semen, by the mere passing back of the locally excessive blood into the ordinary circulatory system. This can happen quite naturally and healthily when the nerves are soothed, either physically or as a result of a sense of mental peace and exaltation. When on the other hand the local excitement culminates in the calling up and expulsion of the semen, after it has once started the ejaculation becomes quite involuntary and the spermatozoa and the secretions associated with them pass out of the system and are entirely lost.

Of what does this loss consist? It is estimated that there are about two hundred and fifty million spermatozoa in a single average ejaculation.[1] Each single one of these (in healthy men) is capable of fertilizing a woman's egg-cell and giving rise to a new human being. (Thus by a single ejaculation one man might fertilize nearly all the marriageable women in the world.)[2] Each single one of those minute spermatozoa carries countless hereditary traits, and each consists very largely of nuclear plasm – the most highly specialized and richest substance in our bodies.

It is therefore the greatest mistake to imagine that the semen is something to be got rid of frequently – all the vital energy and the precious chemical substances which go to its composition can be better utilized by being transformed into other creative work on most days of the month. And so mystic and wonderful are the chemical transformations going on in our bodies that the brain can often set this alchemy in motion, particularly if the brain is helped by knowledge. A strong will can often calm the nerves which regulate the blood supply, and order the distended veins of the penis to retract and subside without wasting the semen in an ejaculation.

But while it is good that a man should be able to do this often, it is not good to try to do it always. The very restraint which adds to a man's strength up to a certain point, taxes his strength when carried beyond it. It is my belief that just sufficient restraint to carry him through the ebb-tides of his wife's sex-rhythm is usually the right amount to give the best strength, vigor, and joy to a man, if both are normal people. If the wife has, as I think the majority of healthy well-fed young women will be found to have, a fortnightly consciousness or potentiality of desire, then the two should find a perfect mutual adjustment in having fortnightly unions; for this need not be confined to only a single union on each occasion. Many men who can well practice restraint for twelve or fourteen days, will find that one union only will not then thoroughly satisfy them; and if they have the good fortune to have healthy wives, they will find that the latter, too, have the desire for several unions in the course of a day or two. If the wave-crests on our charts are studied it will be seen that they spread over two or three days and show several small minor crests. This is what happens when a woman is thoroughly well and vital; her desire bubbles up during a day or two, sometimes even every few hours if it does not, and sometimes even if it does, receive satisfaction.

Expressed in general terms (which, of course, will not fit everybody) my view may be formulated thus: The mutually best regulation of intercourse in marriage is to have three or four days of repeated unions, followed by about ten days without any unions at all, unless some strong external stimulus has stirred a mutual desire.

I have been interested to discover that the people known to me who have accidentally fixed upon this arrangement of their lives are happy: and it should be noted that it fits in with the charts I give which represent the normal, spontaneous feeling of so many women.

There are many women, however, who do not feel, or who may not at first recognize, a second, but have only one time of natural pleasure in sex in each moon-month. Many men of strong will and temperate lives will be able so to control themselves that they can adjust themselves to this more restrained sex-life, as do some with whom I am acquainted. On the other hand, there will be many who find this period too long to live through without using a larger amount of energy in restraining their impulse than is justifiable. It seems to me never justifiable to spend so much energy and will power on restraining natural impulses, that valuable work and intellectual power and poise are made to suffer. If, then, a strongly sexed husband, who finds it a real loss to his powers of work to endure through twenty-six days of abstinence, should find himself married to a wife whose vitality is so low that she can only take pleasure in physical union once in her moon-month (in some it will be before, in some a little time after, her menstrual flow), he should note carefully the time she is spontaneously happy in their union, and then at any cost restrain himself through the days immediately following, and about a fortnight after her time of desire he should set himself ardently to woo her. Unless she is actually out of health he is more likely then than at any other time to succeed not only in winning her compliance, but also in giving her enjoyment and attaining mutual ecstasy.

The husband who so restrains himself, even if it is hard to do it, will generally find that he is a thousandfold repaid – not only by the increasing health and happiness of his wife, and the much intenser pleasure he gains from their mutual intercourse, but also by his own added vitality and sense of self-command. A fortnight is not too long for a healthy man to restrain himself with advantage.

Sir Thomas Clouston says ("Before I Wed," p. 84): *"Nature has so arranged matters that the more constantly control is exercised the more easy and effective it becomes. It becomes a habit. The less control is exercised, the greater tendency there is for a desire to become a craving of an uncontrollable kind, which is itself of the nature of disease, and means death sooner or later."* This conclusion is not only the result of the intellectual and moral experience of our race, but is supported by physiological experiments.

While a knowledge of the fundamental laws of our being should in the main regulate our lives, so complex are we, so sensitive to a myriad impressions, that clock-work regularity can never rule us.

Even where the woman is strongly sexed, with a well-marked recurrence of desire, which is generally satisfied by fortnightly unions, it may not infrequently happen that, in between these periods, there may be additional special occasions when there springs up a mutual longing to unite. These will generally depend on some event in the lovers' lives which stirs their emotions; some memory of past passion, such as an anniversary of their wedding, or perhaps will be due to a novel, poem, or picture which moves them deeply. If the man she loves plays the part of tender wooer, even at times when her passion would not spontaneously arise, a woman can generally be stirred so fundamentally as to give a passionate return. But at the times of her ebb-tides the stimulus will have to be stronger than at the high tides, and it will then generally be found that the appeal must be made even more through her emotional and spiritual nature and less through the physical than usual.

The supreme law for husbands is: Remember that each act of union must be tenderly wooed for and won, and that no union should ever take place unless the woman also desires it and is made physically ready for it.

While in most marriages the husband has to restrain himself to meet the wife's less frequently recurrent rhythm, there are, on the other hand, marriages in which the husband is so under-sexed that he cannot have ordinary union save at very infrequent intervals without a serious effect on his health. If such a man is married to a woman who has inherited an unusually strong and over-frequent desire, he may suffer by union with her, or may cause her suffering by refusing to unite. In such cases we are helpless. We have to deal with one of the many marital tragedies. Unfortunately, the variations in the sex-need of different healthy people is immense, far greater than can be suggested in this book.[3] Indeed the "normal" is rarer than the variations upon it.

Ellis states that the Queen of Aragon ordained that six times a day was the proper rule in legitimate marriage. So abnormally sexed a woman would to-day probably succeed in killing by exhaustion a succession of husbands, for the man who could match such a desire is very rare now-a-days.

Though the timing and the frequency of union are the points about which questions are oftenest asked by the ignorant and well-meaning, and are most misunderstood, yet there are other fundamental facts concerning coitus about which even medical men seem surprisingly ignorant. Regarding these, a simple statement of the physiological facts is essential.

An impersonal and scientific knowledge of the structure of our bodies is the surest safeguard against prurient curiosity and lascivious gloating. This knowledge at the back of the minds of the lovers, though not perhaps remembered as such, may also spare the unintentioned cruelty of handling which so readily injures one whose lover is ignorant.

What actually happens in an act of union should be known. After the preliminaries of love-play, the stimulated penis, erect, enlarged and stiffened, is pressed into the woman's vagina. Ordinarily when a woman is not stimulated, the walls of this canal, as well as the exterior lips of soft tissue surrounding its exit, are dry and rather crinkled, and the vaginal opening is smaller than the man's extended organ. But when the woman is what is physiologically called tumescent (that is, when she is ready for union and has been profoundly stirred), these parts are all flushed by the internal blood supply and to some extent are turgid like those of the man, while there is a plentiful secretion of mucus, which lubricates the channel of the vagina. In a really ardent woman the vagina may even spontaneously open and close as though panting with longing. (So powerful is the influence of thought on our bodily structure, that in some people all these physical results may be brought about by the thought of the loved one, by the enjoyment of tender words and kisses, and the beautiful subtleties of wooing.) It can therefore be readily imagined that when the man tries to enter a woman whom he has not wooed to the point of stimulating her natural physical reactions of preparation, he is endeavoring to force his entry through a dry-walled opening too small for it. He may thus cause the woman actual pain, apart from the mental revolt and loathing she is likely to feel for a man who so regardlessly uses her. On the other hand, in the tumescent woman the opening, already naturally expanded, is lubricated by a flow of mucus, and all the nerves and muscles are ready to react and easily draw in the man's entering organ.

This account is of the meeting of two who have been already married. The first union of a virgin girl differs, of course, from all others, for on that occasion the hymen is broken. One would think that every girl who was about to be married would be told of this necessary rupturing of the membrane and the temporary pain it will cause her; but even still large numbers of girls are allowed to marry in complete and cruel ignorance.

It should be realized that a man does not woo and win a woman once for all when he marries her: he must woo her before every separate act of coitus; for each act corresponds to a marriage, as the beasts of the field and the fowls of the air know it. Wild animals are not so foolish as man; a wild animal does not unite with his female without the wooing characteristic of his race, whether by stirring her by a display of his strength in fighting another male, or by exhibiting his beautiful feathers or song. And we must not forget that the wild animals are assisted by nature; they generally only woo just at the season when the female is beginning to feel natural desire. But man, who wants his mate all out of season as well as in it, has a double duty to perform, and must himself rouse, charm, and stimulate her to the local readiness which would have been to some extent naturally prepared for him had he waited till her own desire welled up.

To render a woman ready before uniting with her is not only the merest act of humanity to save her pain, but is of value from the man's point of view, for (unless he is one of those relatively few abnormal and diseased variants who delight only in rape) the man gains an immense increase of sensation from the mutuality thus attained. [See note at end of book.]

When the two have met and united, the usual result is that, after a longer or shorter interval, the man's mental and physical stimulation reaches a climax in sensory intoxication and in the ejaculation of semen. Where the two are perfectly adjusted, the woman simultaneously reaches the crisis of nervous reactions and muscular convulsions similar to his. This mutual orgasm is extremely important, but in distressingly many cases the man's climax comes so swiftly that the woman's reactions are not nearly ready, and she is left without it.

Though in some instances the woman may have one or more crises before the man achieves his, it is perhaps hardly an exaggeration to say that 70 or 80 per cent. of our married women (in the middle and intellectual classes) are deprived of the full orgasm through the excessive speed of the husband's reactions, i.e., through premature ejaculation (ejaculatio precox) or through some mal-adjustment of the relative shapes and positions of the organs. So complex, so profound, are woman's sex-instincts that in rousing them the man is rousing her whole body and soul. And this takes time. More time indeed than the average husband dreams of spending upon it. Yet woman has at the surface a small vestigial organ called the clitoris, which corresponds morphologically to the man's penis, and which, like it, is extremely sensitive to touch-sensations. This little crest, which lies anteriorly between the inner lips round the vagina, erects itself when the woman is really tumescent, and by the stimulation of movement it is intensely roused and transmits this stimulus to every nerve in her body. But even after a woman's dormant sex-feeling is aroused and all the complex reactions of her being have been set in motion, it may take from ten to twenty minutes of actual physical union to consummate her feeling, while one, two or three minutes of actual union often satisfies a man who is ignorant of the art of controlling his reactions so that he may experience the added enjoyment of a mutual simultaneous orgasm.

A number of well-meaning people demand from men absolute "continence" save for procreation only. They overlook the innumerable physiological reactions concerned in the act, as well as the subtle spiritual alchemy of it, and propound the view that "the opposition to continence, save for procreation only, has but one argument to put forward, and that is appetite, selfishness." (Mary Teats, "The Way of God in Marriage.")

It should be realized, however, that the complete act of union is a triple consummation. It symbolizes, and at the same time actually enhances, the spiritual union; there are a myriad subtleties of soul-structure which are compounded in this alchemy. At the same time the act gives the most intense physical pleasure which the body can experience, and it is a mutual, not a selfish, pleasure, more calculated than anything else to draw out an unspeakable tenderness and understanding in both partakers of this sacrament; while, thirdly, it is the act which gives rise to a new life by rendering possible the fusion of one of the innumerable male spermatozoa with the female egg-cell.

It often happens, now-a-days, that dreading the expense and the physical strain of child-bearing for his wife, the husband practices what is called coitus interruptus: that is, he withdraws just before the ejaculation, but when he is already so stimulated that the ejaculation has become involuntary. In this way the semen is spent, but, as it does not enter the wife's body, fertilization and consequently procreation cannot take place. This practice, while it may have saved the woman the anguish of bearing unwanted children, is yet very harmful to her, and is to be deprecated. It tends to leave the woman in "mid-air" as it were; to leave her stimulated and unsatisfied, and therefore it has a very bad effect on her nerves and general health, particularly if it is done frequently. The woman, too, loses the advantage (and I am convinced that it is difficult to overstate the physiological advantage) of the partial absorption of the man's secretions, which must take place through the large tract of internal epithelium with which they come in contact. If, as physiology has already proved to be the case, the internal absorption of secretions from the sex organs plays so large a part in determining the health and character of remote parts of the body, it is extremely likely that the highly stimulating secretion of man's semen can and does penetrate and affect the woman's whole organism. Actual experiment has shown that iodine placed in the vagina in solution is so quickly absorbed by the epithelial walls that in an hour it has penetrated the system and is even being excreted. It still remains, however, for scientific experiments to be devised which will enable us to study the effects of the absorption of substances from the semen. On the other hand, coitus interruptus is not always harmful for the man, for he has the complete sex-act, though a good many men think its effects on them are undesirable, and it may lead to lack of desire or even impotence. It is certainly bad when its safety from consequences induces him to frequent indulgence, for thus wastefully to scatter what should be creative power is to reduce his own vitality and power of work. By those who have a high appreciation of the value of their creative impulse, and who wish to enjoy the mutual pleasure and enhancement of sex-union without wasting it, this method should not be practiced.

[Personal experience with thousands of men and hundreds of women who have been the victims of coitus interruptus, coitus incompletus or coitus prolongatus entitles the editor to speak with authority on the subject. It is hard to determine who, the man or the woman, is more seriously, more extensively injured by the practice; but my own impression is that it is the man. While, as a result of the practice, both may become afflicted with a lack of libido, or even a distaste and loathing of sex relations, tachycardia, neurasthenia, etc., there is one condition which may and often does affect the man, but from which the woman remains free, and that is: impotentia coeundi. Atony and congestion of the prostate are also conditions from which the man alone suffers.

As to absorption of the semen by the female genitals, no scientific proof exists that even absorption takes place. Of the absorption by the vaginal epithelium there can be no question; there is some likelihood of absorption by the epithelium of the lining membrane of the uterus. But even here scientific proof is still lacking. The absorption of one's own internal secretions is not an analogous case: Here the secretion is poured directly into one's own blood or lymph stream. But it is a fact that many women suffer intensely when in their sex relations they are deprived of the semen, either through the practice of coitus interruptus or through the use of a condom. W. J. R.]

It should never be forgotten that without the discipline of control there is no lasting delight in erotic feeling. The fullest delight, even in a purely physical sense, can only be attained by those who curb and direct their natural impulses.

Dr. Saleeby's words are appropriate in this connection (Introduction to Forel's "Sexual Ethics"): "*Professor Forel speaks of subduing the sexual instinct. I would rather speak of transmuting it. The direct method of attack is often futile, always necessitous of effort, but it is possible for us to transmute our sex-energy into higher forms in our individual lives, thus justifying the evolutionary and physiological contention that is the source of the higher activities of man, of moral indignation, and of the 'restless energy' which has changed the surface of the earth.*"

Forel says ("The Sexual Question"): "*Before engaging in a life-long union, a man and woman ought to explain to each other their sexual feelings so as to avoid deception and incompatibility later on.*" This would be admirable advice were it possible for a virgin girl to know much about the reactions and effects upon her mind and body of the act of coitus, but she does not. Actually it often takes several years for eager and intelligent couples fully to probe themselves and to discover the extent and meaning of the immensely profound physiological and spiritual results of marriage. Yet it is true that a noble frankness would save much misery when, as happens not infrequently, one or other of the pair marries with the secret determination not to have any children.

So various are we all as individuals, so complex all the reactions and later-reactions of sex relations, that no hard and fast rule can be laid down. Each couple, after marriage, must study themselves, and the lover and the beloved must do what best serves them both and gives them the highest degree of mutual joy and power. There are, however, some laws which should be inviolable. Their details can be gathered from the preceding pages, and they are summed up in the words: *"Love worketh no ill to the beloved."*

Footnotes

1. See Pflüger's Archiv., 1891.

2. This is less utterly fantastic than it may sound, now that science has taught us how to fertilize females by semen from males they may never have seen.

3. On this point the reader may consult Dr. Robinson's "Treatise on Sexual Impotence and Other Sexual Disorders in Men and Women."

Sleep

"He giveth His beloved sleep."

THE healing magic of sleep is known to all.

Sleeplessness is a punishment for so many different violations of nature's laws, that it is perhaps one of the most prevalent of humanity's innumerable sufferings. While most of the aspects of sleep and sleeplessness have received much attention from specialists in human physiology, the relation between sleep and coitus appears to be but little realized. Yet there is an intimate, profound and quite direct relation between the power of sleep, naturally and refreshingly, and the harmonious relief of the whole system in the perfected sex-act.

We see this very clearly in the case of the ordinary healthy man. If, for some reason, he has to live unsatisfied for some time after the acute stirring of his longing for physical contact with his wife, he tends in the interval to be wakeful, restless, and his nerves are on edge.

Then, when the propitious hour arrives, and after the love-play, the growing passion expands, until the transports of rapture find their ending in the explosive completion of the act, at once the tension of his whole system relaxes, and his muscles fall into gentle, easy attitudes of languorous content, and in a few moments the man is sleeping like a child.

This excellent and refreshing sleep falls like a soft curtain of oblivion and saves the man's consciousness from the jar and disappointment of an anti-climax. But not only is this sleep a restorative after the strenuous efforts of the transport, it has peculiarly refreshing powers, and many men feel that after such a sleep their whole system seems rejuvenated.

But how fare women in this event? When they too have had complete satisfaction they similarly relax and sink into a peaceful refreshing slumber.

But as things are to-day it is scarcely an exaggeration to say that the majority of wives are left wakeful and nerve-racked to watch with tender motherly brooding, or with bitter and jealous envy, the slumbers of the men who, through ignorance and carelessness, have neglected to see that they too received full satisfaction.

Many married women have told me that after relations with their husbands they are restless, either for some hours or for the whole night; and I feel sure that the prevalent neglect on the part of men to see that their wives have orgasms at each congress, must be a very common source of the sleeplessness and nervous diseases of so many married women.

The relation between the completion of the sex-act and sleep in woman is well indicated in the case of Mrs. A. who is typical of a large class of wives. She married a man with whom she was passionately in love. Neither she nor her husband had ever had connection with any one else, and, while they were both keen and intelligent people with some knowledge of biology, neither knew anything of the details of human sex union. For several years her husband had unions with her which gave him some satisfaction and left him ready at once to sleep. Neither he nor she knew that women should have an orgasm, and after every union she was left so "on edge," restless and wakeful, so that several hours would generally elapse before she could sleep at all, and often she remained wakeful the whole night.

After her husband's death her health improved, and in a year or two she entered into a new relation with a man who was aware of woman's needs and gave sufficient time and attention to them to ensure a successful orgasm for her as well as for himself. The result was that she soon became a good sleeper, with the attendant benefits of restored nerves and health.

Sleep is so complex a process, and sleeplessness the resultant of so many different mal-adjustments, that it is, of course, possible that the woman may sleep well enough, even if she be deprived of the relief and pleasure of perfect union. But in so many married women sleeplessness and a consequent nervous condition are coupled with a lack of the complete sex relation, that one of the first questions a physician should put to those of his women patients who are worn and sleepless is whether her husband really fulfills his marital duty in their physical relation.

From their published statements, and their admissions to me, it appears that many practicing doctors are either almost unaware of the very existence of orgasm in women, or look upon it as a superfluous and accidental phenomenon. Yet to have had a moderate number of orgasms at some time at least, is a necessity for the full development of a woman's health and all her powers.

As this book is written for those who are married, I say nothing here about the lives of those who are still unmarried, though, particularly after the age of thirty has been reached, their case may be very sad and need much study and consideration. It is, however, worth noticing how prevalent sleeplessness is among a class of women who have never practiced any self-indulgence or allowed any relief to their desires. There is little doubt that the complete lack of normal sex relations is one of the several factors which render many middle-aged unmarried women nervous and sleepless.

Yet for the unmarried woman the lack is not so acute nor so localized as it is for the married woman who is thwarted in the natural completion of her sex-functions after they have been directly stimulated.

The unmarried woman, unless she be in love with some particular man, has no definite stimulus to her sex desires beyond the natural upwelling of the sex urge. The married woman, however, is not only diffusely stirred by the presence of the man she loves, but is also acutely, locally and physically, stimulated by his relation with her.

And if she is then left in mid air, without natural relief to her tension, she is in this respect far worse off than her unmarried sister.

Nevertheless, many unmarried women suffer from sleeplessness as a result of their celibacy, quite unconscious of its cause.

We are, however, only concerned here with the married woman. When she is left sleepless through the neglect of the mate who slumbers soundly by her side, it is not surprising if she spends the long hours reviewing their mutual position; and the review cannot yield her much pleasure or satisfaction. For deprived of the physical delight of mutual orgasm (though, perhaps, like so many wives, quite unconscious of all it can give), she sees in the sex act an arrangement where pleasure, relief and subsequent sleep are all on her husband's side, while she is merely the passive instrument of his enjoyment. Nay, more than that: if following every union she has long hours of wakefulness, she then sees clearly the encroachment on her own health of an arrangement in which she is not merely passive, but is actively abused.

Another of the consequences of the incomplete relation is that often, stirred to a point of wakefulness and vivacity by the preliminary sex-stimulation (of the full meaning of which she may be unconscious), a romantic and thoughtful woman is then most able to talk intimately and tenderly – to speak of the things most near and sacred to her heart. And she may then be terribly wounded by the inattention of her husband, which, coming so soon after his ardent demonstrations of affection, appears peculiarly callous. It makes him appear to her to be indifferent to the highest side of marriage – the spiritual and romantic intercourse. Thus she may see in the man going off to sleep in the midst of her love-talk, a gross and inattentive brute – and all because she has never shared the climax of his physical tension, and does not know that its natural reaction is sleep.

These thoughts are so depressing even to the tenderest and most loving woman, and so bitter to one who has other causes of complaint, that in their turn they act on the whole system and increase the damage done by the mere sleeplessness.

The older school of physiologists dealt in methods too crude to realize the physiological results of our thoughts, but it is now well known that anger and bitterness have experimentally recognizable physiological effects, and are injurious to the whole system.

It requires little imagination to see that after months or years of such embittered sleeplessness, the woman tends not only to become neurasthenic but also resentful towards her husband. She is probably too ignorant and unobservant of her own physiology to realize the full meaning of what is taking place, but she feels vaguely that he is to blame, and that she is being sacrificed for what, in her still greater ignorance of his physiology, seems to her to be his mere pleasure and self-indulgence.

He, with his health maintained by the natural outlet followed by recuperative sleep, is not likely to be ready to look into the gloomy and shadowy land of vague reproach and inexplicable trivial wrongs which are all the expression she gives to her unformulated physical grievance. So he is likely to set down any resentment she may show to "nerves" or "captiousness", and to be first solicitous of and then impatient towards her apparently irrelevant complaints.

If he is, as many men are, tender and considerate, he may try to remedy matters by restricting to the extreme limit of what is absolutely necessary for him, the number of times they come together. Unconsciously he thus only makes matters worse; for as a general rule, he is quite unaware of his wife's rhythm, and does not arrange to coincide with it in his infrequent tender embraces. As he is now probably sleeping in another room and not daring to come for the nightly talks and tenderness which are so sweet a privilege of marriage, here, as in other ways, his well-meaning but wrongly conceived efforts at restraint only tend to drive the pair still further apart.

To make plain the reasonableness of my view regarding sleep, it is necessary to mention some of the immensely profound influences which it is now known that sex exerts, even when not stimulated to its specific use.

In those who are deprived of their sex-organs, particularly when young, many of the other features and organs of the body develop abnormally or fail to appear. Castrated boys (Eunuchs) when grown up, tend to have little or no beard, or mustache, to have high-pitched voices and several other characters which separate them from normal men.

The growth of organs and structures so remote from the sex-organs, as, e.g., the larynx have been found to be influenced by the chemical stimulus of secretions from the sex-organs and their subsidiary glands. These secretions are not passed out through external ducts but enter the blood-system directly. Such secretions passing straight from the ductless glands into the vascular system are of very great importance in almost all our bodily functions. They have been deeply studied of late, and the general name of Hormones given to them by Starling.[1] The idea that some particular secretions or "humors" are connected with each of the internal organs of the body, is a very ancient one; but we have even yet only the vaguest and most elementary knowledge of a few of the many miracles performed by these subtle chemical substances. Thus we know that the stimulus of food in the stomach sends a chemical substance from one ductless gland in the digestive system chasing through the blood to another gland which prepares a different digestive secretion further on. We know that the thyroid gland in the neck swells and contracts in very sensitive relation with the sex organs; we know that some chemical secretion from the developing embryo, or the tissue in which it grows, sends its chemical stimulus to the distant mammary glands of the mother; we know that if the ovaries of a girl or the testes of a boy are completely cut out, the far-reaching influences their hormones would have exerted are made evident by the numerous changes in the system and departures from the normal, which result from their lack.

But we do not know, for physiologists have not yet studied the degree and character of the immense stimulus of sex-life and experience on the glands of the sex-organs, or how they affect the whole of the human being's life and powers.

The "Mendelians" and the "Mutationists," who both tend to lay so much (and I think such undue) stress on morphological hereditary factors, seem at present to have the ear of the public more than the physiologists. But it is more important that every grown up man and woman should know that through the various chemical substances or "messengers" (which Starling calls the hormones) there is an extremely rapid, almost immediate, effect on the activities of organs in remote parts of the body, due to the influences exerted on one or other internal organ.

It is therefore clear that any influences exerted on such profoundly important organs as those connected with sex, must have far-reaching results in many unexpected fields.

What must be taking place in the female system as a result of the completed sex act?

It is true that in coitus woman has but a slight external secretion, and that principally of mucus. But we have no external signs of all the complex processes and reactions going on in digestion and during the production of digestive secretions. When, as is the case in orgasm, we have such intense and apparent nervous, vascular and muscular reactions, it seems inevitable that there must be correspondingly profound internal correlations. Is it conceivable that organs so fundamental, whose mere existence we know affects the personal characters of women, could escape physiological result, from the intense preliminary stimulus and acute sensations of an orgasm?

To ask this question is surely to answer it. It is to my mind inconceivable that the orgasm in woman as in man should not have profound physiological effects. Did we know enough about the subject, many of the "nervous breakdowns" and neurotic tendencies of the modern woman could be directly traced to the partial stimulation of sexual intercourse without its normal completion which is so prevalent in modern marriage.

This subject, and its numerous ramifications, are well worth the careful research of the most highly trained physiologists. There is nothing more profound, or of more vital moment to modern humanity as a whole, than is the understanding of the sex nature and sex needs of men and women.

I may point out as a mere suggestion that the man's sex organs give rise to external and also to internal secretions. The former only leave the glands which secrete them as a result of definite stimulus; the latter appear to be perpetually exuded in small quantities and always to be entering and influencing the whole system. In woman we know there are corresponding perpetual internal secretions, and it seems evident to me that there must be some internal secretions which are only released under the definite stimulus of the whole sex act.

The English and American peoples, who lead the world in so many ways, have an almost unprecedentedly high proportion of married women who get no satisfaction from physical union with their husbands, though they bear children, and may in every other respect appear to be happily married.

The modern civilized neurotic woman has become a by-word in the Western world. Why?

I am certain that much of this suffering is caused by the ignorance of both men and women regarding not only the inner physiology, but even the obvious outward expression, of the complete sex-act.

Many medical men now recognize that numerous nervous and other diseases are associated with the lack of physiological relief for natural or stimulated sex feelings in women. Ellis ("Sex in Relation to Society," 1910, p. 551) quotes the opinion of an Austrian gynecologist who said that, "of every hundred women who come to him with uterine troubles, seventy suffer from congestion of the womb, which he regarded as due to incomplete coitus." While a writer in the British Medical Journal (April 1, 1911, p. 784) published some cases in which quite serious nervous diseases in wives were put right when their husbands were cured of too hasty ejaculation.

Sleep, concerning which I began this chapter, is but one of innumerable indications of inner processes intimately bound up with the sex-reactions. When the sex-rite is, in every sense, rightly performed, the healing wings of sleep descend both on the man and on the woman in his arms. Every organ in their bodies is influenced and stimulated to play its part, while their spirits, after soaring in the dizzy heights of rapture, are wafted to oblivion, thence to return gently to the ordinary plains of daily consciousness.

Footnotes

1. "See Prof. Ernest H. Starling's Croonian Lecture to the Royal Society, 1905.

Modesty and Romance

"A person can therefore no more promise to love or not to love than he can promise to live long. What he can promise is to take good care of his life and of his love."

–Ellen Key.

ARTISTS clearly, and poets in veiled language, have in all ages expressed the glory of the naked human body. Before the Venus of Milo in her Paris home, even the empty-headed and ridiculously dressed creatures of fashion stand for a moment with a catch in the throat and a sense that here is something full of divine secrets. One day, when I was doing my reverence before this ancient goddess, drinking in strength and happiness from the harmonies of her curves, a preposterously corseted doll came up to the statue, paused, and said with tears in her voice to the man beside her: "Hasn't she got the loveliest figure! "

If cold marble so stirs us, how much more the warmth and vitality of living beauty! Any well-formed young man or woman is immeasurably more graceful when free from the clinging follies of modern dress, while a beautiful woman's body has a supernal loveliness at which no words short of poetic rapture can even hint. What wonder then that one of the ecstasies of love should be the unveiling of the beloved?

A man or woman perfectly naked cannot be tawdry. The fripperies, the jagged curves and inharmonious lines and colors of the so-called "adornments" are surmounted, and the naked figure stepping from their scattered pile is seen in its utter simplicity. How charming even the raggedest little street urchins become when they leave their rags on the bank and plunge into the water!

It is therefore not surprising that one of the innumerable sweet impulses of love should be to reveal, each to each, this treasure of living beauty: To give each other the right to enter and enjoy the sight which most of all sights in the world draws and satisfies the artist's eyes.

This impulse, however, is, on the part of the woman, swayed by two at least of the natural results of her rhythmic tides. For some time during each month, age-long tradition that she is "unclean," coupled with her obvious requirements, have made her withdraw herself from even her husband's gaze. But, on the other hand, there regularly comes the time before menstruation when her body is raised to a higher point of loveliness than usual by the rounding and extra fullness of the breasts. (This is one of the regular physiological results of the processes going on within her, of which menstruation is only the outward sign.) Partly or wholly unconscious of the brilliance and full perfection of her beauty, she yet delights in its gentle promptings to reveal itself to her lover's eyes when he adores. This innocent, this goddess-like self-confidence retreats when the natural ebb of her vitality returns.

How fortunate for man when these sweet changes in his beloved are not coerced into uniformity! For man has still so much of the ancient hunter in his blood that beauty which is always at hand and ever upon its pedestal must inevitably attract him far less than the elusive and changing charms of rhythmic life. In the highly evolved and cultivated woman, who has wisdom enough not to restrict, but to give full play to the great rhythms of her being, man's polygamous instinct can be satisfied and charmed by the ever-changing aspects of herself which naturally come uppermost. And one of her natural phases is at times to retreat, to experience a profound sex indifference, and passionately to resent any encroachment on her solitude.

This is something woman too often forgets. She has been so thoroughly "domesticated" by man that she feels too readily that after marriage she is all his. And by her very docility to his perpetual demands she destroys for him the elation, the palpitating thrills and surprises, of the chase.

In the rather trivial terms of our sordid modern life, it works out in many marriages somewhat as follows: The married pair share a bedroom, often even a bed (though this detestable habit is fortunately rapidly decreasing) and so it comes about that the two are together not only at the times of delight and interest in each other, but during most of the unlovely and even ridiculous proceedings of the toilet. Now it may enchant a man once – perhaps even twice – or at long intervals – to watch his goddess screw her hair up into a tight and unbecoming knot and soap her ears. But it is inherently too unlovely a proceeding to retain indefinite enchantment. To see her floating in the deep, clear water of her bath – that may enchant for ever, for it is so lovely, but the unbeautiful trivialities essential to the cleaning processes of a bath, tend only to dim the picture and, if repeated, to dull the interest and attention that should be bestowed on the body of the loved one. Hence, ultimately, everyday association in the commonplace daily necessities tends to reduce the keen pleasure each takes in the sight of the other. And hence, inevitably and tragically though stealthily and unperceived, to reduce the keenness of stimulation the pair exert on each other, and thus to lower their intensity of pleasure in the sex act.[1]

In short, the overcoming of her personal modesty which is generally looked on as an essential result in marriage where the woman becomes wholly the man's, has generated among our women a tradition that before their husbands they can perform any and all of the details of personal and domestic duties. Correspondingly, they allow the man to be neglectful of preserving some reticence before them. This mutual possession of the lower and more elementary experiences of life has been, in innumerable marriages, a factor in destroying the mutual possession of life's higher and more poetic charms.

In this respect I am inclined to think that man suffers more than woman. For man is still essentially the hunter, the one who experiences the desires and thrills of the chase, and dreams ever of coming unawares upon Diana in the woodlands. On the other hand, the married woman, having once yielded all, tends to remain passively in the man's companionship.

Though it may appear trivial beside the profound physiological factors considered in recent chapters, I think that, in the interest of husbands, an important piece of advice to wives is: Be always escaping. Escape the lower, the trivial, the sordid. So far as possible (and this is far more possible than appears at first, and requires only a little care and rearrangement in the habits of the household) ensure that you allow your husband to come upon you only when there is delight in the meeting. A fleeting glimpse of mutinous face as you lock yourself in the bathroom, is far kinder to a man than the wifely docility of sharing a toilet table and washstand.

Footnotes

1. A quotation from W. J. Thomas, "Sex and Society," is here very apt, though he had been speaking not of man, but of the love-play and coyness shown by female birds and animals. "We must also recognize the fact that reproductive life must be connected with violent stimulation, or it would be neglected and the species would become extinct; and on the other hand if the conquest of the female were too easy, sexual life would be in danger of becoming a play interest and a dissipation, destructive of energy and fatal to the species. Working, we may assume, by a process of selection and survival, nature has both secured and safeguarded reproduction. The female will not submit to seizure except in a high state of nervous excitation (as is seen especially well in the wooing of birds), while the male must conduct himself in such a way as to manipulate the female and, as the more active agent, he develops a marvellous display of technique for this purpose. This is offset by the coyness and coquetry of the female, by which she equally attracts and fascinates the male, and practices upon him to induce a corresponding state of nervous excitation."

Abstinence

"How intoxicating indeed, how penetrating – like a most precious wine – is that love which is the sexual transformed by the magic of the will into the emotional and spiritual! And what a loss on the merest grounds of prudence and the economy of pleasure is its unbridled waste along physical channels! So nothing is so much to be dreaded between lovers as just this – the vulgarization of love – and this is the rock upon which marriage so often splits."

–Edward Carpenter

AND because marriage so often splits upon this rock, or because men and women have in all ages yearned for spiritual beauty, there have been those who shut themselves off from all the sweet usages of the body. In the struggle of man to gain command over his body, and in the slow and often backsliding evolution of the higher love, there is no doubt that humanity owes much to the ascetic. But this debt is in the past. We are now gaining control of the lower forces, we are winning knowledge of the complex meanings and the spiritual transformations of our physical reactions, and in the future the highest social unit will be recognized to be the pair, fused in love so that all human potentialities are theirs, as well as the higher potentialities which only perfect love can originate.

Yet, as we live to-day, with still so many remnants of the older standards within and upon us, we must endeavor to understand the ascetic. He (less often she) is by no means seldom one of the products of marriage. It not infrequently happens that after a love-marriage and some years of what is considered happiness, the man or woman may withdraw from the sex-life, often looking down upon it, and considering that they have reached a higher plane by so doing. But such people seldom ask themselves if, while they lived it, they reached the highest possible level of the sex-life.

One of the most famous instances of the married ascetic is Tolstoy, whose later opinion was that the highest human being completely inhibits his sex-desires and lives a celibate life. Ascetics, however, seldom have much knowledge of human physiology, and it seems to me that, with all their fine and religious fervor, they often lack the mysticism necessary for the full realization of the meaning and potentialities of the new creation resulting from man's and woman's highest union. Doubtless if for an hour we were to take the place of the individual chemical atoms of Oxygen or of Hydrogen, we could have no inkling of the physical properties of the water-drop they together form.

Christianity, like most religions, had a strong wave of asceticism early in its history. While there was, as there still is, a harsh asceticism which is hostile to the other sex, it is of much interest to see that there was also a romantic asceticism which, while revolting from the sensuality of its pagan contemporaries, did not entirely prohibit the charms and pleasures of mutual companionship. Thus, in a mutilated form, it seems, these early Christian ascetics gained some of the immaterial benefits of marriage. Ellis ("Sex and Society") gives an interesting account of these ascetic love-unions:

> "Our fathers," Chrysostom begins ("Against those who keep Virgins in their Houses"), "only knew two forms of sexual intimacy, marriage and fornication. Now a third form has appeared: men introduce young girls into their houses and keep them there permanently, respecting their virginity. What," Chrysostom asks, "is the reason? It seems to me that life in common with a woman is sweet, even outside conjugal union and fleshly commerce. That is my feeling; and perhaps it is not my feeling alone; it may also be that of these men. They would not hold their honor so cheap nor give rise to such scandals if this pleasure were not violent and tyrannical. . . . That there should really be a pleasure in this which produces a love more ardent than conjugal union may surprise you at first. But when I give you the proofs you will agree that it is so." The absence of restraint to desire in marriage, he continues, often leads to speedy disgust, and

even apart from this, sexual intercourse, pregnancy, delivery, lactation, the bringing up of children, and all the pains and anxieties that accompany these things, soon destroy youth and dull the point of pleasure. The virgin is free from these burdens. She retains her vigor and her youthfulness, and even at the age of forty may rival the young nubile girl. "A double ardor thus burns in the heart of him who lives with her, and the gratification of desire never extinguishes the bright flame which ever continues to increase in strength." Chrysostom describes minutely all the little cares and attentions which the modern girls of his time required, and which these men delighted to expend on their virginal sweethearts whether in public or in private. He cannot help thinking, however, that the man who lavishes kisses and caresses on a woman whose virginity he retains is putting himself somewhat in the position of Tantalus. But this new refinement of tender chastity, which came as a delicious discovery to the early Christians who resolutely thrust away the licentiousness of the pagan world, was deeply rooted, as we discover from the frequency with which the grave Fathers of the Church, apprehensive of scandal, felt called upon to reprove it, though their condemnation is sometimes not without a trace of secret sympathy. hus Jerome, in his letter to Eustochium, refers to those couples who 'share the same room,' often even the same bed, and call us suspicious if we draw any conclusions; while Cyprian (Epistola, 86) is unable to approve of those men he hears of, one a deacon, who live in familiar intercourse with virgins, even sleeping in the same bed with them, for, he declares, the feminine sex is weak and youth is wanton."

The harsh ascetic, however, is the one the word ascetic most generally conjures up. Even if he accomplishes miracles of self-restraint, and subdues desire, he is often weakened rather than strengthened by his determination to flout nature. Save only in the truly great, there is a warping and narrowing which results from coercing beyond the limits of reason the desires which were implanted in Adam and Eve when they were told to be fruitful and multiply.

As Ellen Key says ("Love and Marriage"):

> "Those ascetics who recommend only self-control as a remedy for the mastery of sexual instinct, even when such control becomes merely obstructive to life, are like the physician who tried only to drive the fever out of his patient: it was nothing to him that the sick man died of the cure. But these ascetics may have arrived at their fanaticism by two different paths. One group – which includes most of the female ascetics – hates Cupid because he has never shown to them any favor. The other group – embracing the majority of male ascetics – curses him because he never leaves them in peace."

Approaching the subject in a more modern and scientific attitude of impartial inquiry, the medical man can produce an imposing list of diseases[1] more or less directly caused by abstinence both in men and in women. These diseases range from neuralgia and "nerves" to actual fibroid growths. And it is well worthy of remark that these diseases may be present when the patient (as have many unmarried women) has no idea that the sex impulse exists unmastered.

Thus the ascetic and the profligate (whether or not in legal marriage) have both to run the gauntlet of disease. There is, however, no disease I know of which is caused by the normal and mutually happy marriage relation – a relation which, certainly to most has positive healing and vitalizing power.

The profound truth which is perceived by the ascetics is that the creative energy of sex can be transformed into other activities. This truth should never be lost sight of in marriage; the periods of complete abstinence, between the times of natural, happy, and also stimulating exercise of the sex-functions, should be opportunities for transmuting the healthy sex-power into work of every sort.

Footnotes

1. I should prefer to use the word "disorders" instead of diseases. As to fibroid tumors as a result of abstinence – no scientific authentic data are available on this point.

Children

I am for you, and you are for me, Not only for your own sake, but for others' sakes, Envelop'd in you sleep greater heroes and bards, They refuse to awake at the touch of any man but me.

-Walt Whitman.

THE Mystic in his moment of enlightenment attains through the flux of his personality the realization of oneness with the divine forces of the Universe.

To ordinary men and women, however, this mystical ecstasy is unknown, and the ordinary human consciousness is far more aware of its separateness than of its oneness with the vital forces of creation. Yet the glow of half-swooning rapture in which the Mystic's whole being melts and floats in the light of the divine force is paralleled in the rapture of lovers.

When two who are mated in every respect burn with the fire of the innumerable forces within them, which set their bodies longing toward each other with the desire to inter-penetrate and to encompass one another, the fusion joy and rapture is not purely physical. The half swooning sense of flux which overtakes the spirit in that moment at the apex of rapture sweeps into its tides the whole essence of the man and woman, and as it were, the heat of the contact vaporizes their consciousness so that it fills the whole of cosmic space. For the moment they are identified with the divine thoughts, the waves of eternal force, which to the Mystic often appear in terms of golden light.

From their mutual penetration into the realms of supreme joy the two lovers bring back with them a spark of that light which we call life.

And unto them a child is born.

This is the supreme purpose of nature in all her enticing weft of complex factors, luring the two lovers into each other's arms. Only by the fusion of two can the new human life come into being, and only by creating a new life in this way can we hand on the torch which lights our consciousness in the sphere of matter.

This mystical and wonderful fact has never yet found the poet to sing its full glory. But in the hearts of all who have known true love lies the realization of the sacredness that is theirs when they are in the very act of creation.

Were our bodies specifically organized for this supreme purpose, two human beings would only pass through the sacred fire of mutual fusion in order to create a new life. But, however far our spirits have evolved, our bodies are composed of matter which bears the imprint of the many past phases through which we have reached our present position. And because in the world of the lower animals there is an immense wastage of all the young lives created, and it is necessary that myriads should be conceived in order that a small number should reach maturity, so in our bodies (specialized though they are in comparison with the lower animals) both sexes still produce a far larger number of germs awaiting fertilization than can be actually fructified and imbued with individual life.

It is utterly impossible, organized as our bodies are at present, for us to obey the dictates of theologians and refrain from the wasting of potential life. The germ cells of the woman, though immeasurably less numerous than the male germ cells (the spermatozoa), yet develop uselessly over and over again in every celibate as well as in every married woman. And myriads of sperm cells are destroyed even in the process of the act which does ensure fertilization of the woman by the single favored spermatozoön. If the theologians really mean what they say, and demand the voluntary effort of complete celibacy from all men, save for the purpose of procreation, this will not achieve their end of preventing the wastage of all potential life; and the monthly loss of unfertilized ova by women is beyond all the efforts of the will to curb. Nature, not man, arranged the wastage of potential life against which ascetic bishops rage.

If, then, throughout the greater part of their lives the germinal cells of both sexes inevitably disintegrate without creating an embryo, there can be nothing wrong in selecting the most favorable moment possible for the conception of a new life.

What generally happens in marriage where this is not thought of is that one of the very earliest unions results in the fertilization of the wife, so that the young pair have a baby nine months, or a little more, after marriage.

Whereas, were they wise and did they realize the full significance of what they were doing, they would allow at least six months or a year to elapse before beginning the supreme task of their lives, the burden of which falls mainly upon the woman.

For many reasons it is more ideal to have the children spontaneously and early; but if economic conditions are hard, as they so often are in "civilized" life, it may be better to marry and defer the children rather than not to marry.

If the pair married very young, and before they could afford to support children, they might wait several years with advantage. An exceptional case is one of the happiest marriages I know. The pair married while they were young students in the University, and fourteen years later they had their first child, a splendidly healthy boy. Though such a long interval is certainly not to be universally recommended, as it is said that it may result in sterility [preventive measures in themselves never lead to sterility. W. J. R.], in this instance it was triumphantly better for the two to have lived normally satisfied happy lives than to have waited for fourteen years, and risked the man's "fall."

There are many reasons, both for their own and for the child's sake, why the potential parents should take the wise precaution of delay, unless owing to special circumstances they cannot expect to live together uninterruptedly.

The child, conceived in rapture and hope, should be given every material chance which the wisdom and love of the parents can devise. And the first and most vital condition of its health is that the mother should be well and happy and free from anxiety while she bears it.

The tremendous and far-reaching effects of marriage on the woman's whole organism make her less fitted to bear a child at the very commencement of marriage than later on when the system will have adjusted itself to its new conditions and she will have regained her poise and normal health.

Not only for the sake of the child, however, should the first conception be a little delayed, but also to secure the lasting happiness of the married lovers. It is generally (though perhaps not always) wise thoroughly to establish their relation to each other before introducing the inevitable dislocation and readjustment necessitated by the wife's pregnancy and the birth of a child.

In this book I am not speaking so much of the universal sex relation, as to those who find themselves to-day in the highly civilized, artificial communities of English speaking people: and in our present society there is little doubt that the early birth of a child demands much self-sacrifice and self-restraint from the man, one of the reflex vibrations of which is his undefinable sense of loss and separation from his bride. This has been confided to me by many men who have been generous enough to trust me with some of the secrets of their lives. Mr. C. is typical of many others of his class.

He was quiet and refined with a strong strain of romantic love, which was entirely centered in his bride. He was manly and sufficiently virile to feel the need of sex intercourse, but he was unaware (as are so many men) of the woman's corresponding need; and he did not give his wife any orgasm. She took no pleasure therefore in the physical act of union, which for her was so incomplete.

Very shortly after marriage she conceived, and a child was born ten months after the wedding day.

For two years after the birth of the child her vitality was so lowered that the sex act was to her so repugnant that she refused her husband any union; and it was thus three years after their marriage before they met in anything like a normal way. By that time the long separation from sex-life, and the strain on the man, coupled with daily familiarity at home, had dimmed, if not completely destroyed, his sense of romance. The natural stimulation each should exert on the other had faded, so that they never experienced the mutual glow of intense rapture in their sex-union.

Another pair suffered similarly: Mr. and Mrs. D. were prevented for several years by the wife's real and fancied ill-health from having any intercourse. When, after that time, she recovered and passionately desired the true marriage relation, the husband felt it to be impossible. To him it would have been, as he expressed it, "like raping his sister."

Once such a thought has grown into a man's mind it is very difficult "to recapture the first early rapture." And with the loss of that early rapture the two lose, for the rest of their lives, the irradiating joy which is priceless not only for its beauty but for the vitality with which its wings are laden.

On the other hand, if by waiting some months (or even years if they are young) the mated pair have learnt to adjust themselves to each other and have experienced the full and supreme rapture of complete love-making, the disturbance which is caused by the birth of the child is in no sense a danger to their happiness, but is its crown and completion.

A man once said to me – one can endure anything for the sake of a beloved wife. But the wife is only utterly beloved when she and her married lover have not only entered paradise together, but when she fully realizes, through insight gained by her own experiences, the true nature of that of which she is depriving her husband so long as her bodily condition makes sex-unions with him impossible.

Much has been written, and may be found in the innumerable books on the sex-problems, as to whether a man and woman should or should not have relations while the wife is bearing an unborn child. In this matter experience is very various, so that it is difficult or impossible to give definite advice without knowing the full circumstances of each case.

When, however, we observe the admirable sanctity of the pregnant females of the woodland creatures, and when we consider the extraordinary ignorance and disregard of woman's needs which mark so many of our modern customs, we cannot but think that the safe side of this debatable question must be in the complete continence of the woman for at least six months before the birth of the child. I have heard from a number of women, however, that they desire union urgently at this time, and from others that the thought of it is incredible.

[To demand complete continence for at least six months before the child is born is entirely too severe a requirement. As a woman should for several reasons wait six weeks or two months after the birth of the child before resuming sex relations, it follows that with each pregnancy the husband would have to be abstinent for a period of about eight months. Such complete abstinence would be for some husbands difficult, for some unbearable. For some it might result in very unpleasant complications. Nor is it so easy for all wives during the acme of their sex lives to abstinent for eight months, especially if we bear in mind that with some women the sex-urge is extremely insistent during pregnancy. No, such abstinence is unnecessary. Six weeks to two months of abstinence before and the same period after the birth of a child is quite sufficient, and proper, and will not injure husband, wife or child. – See Chapter: Intercourse During Pregnancy in the Editor's "Women – Her Sex and Love Life." W. J. R.]

Tolstoy strongly condemned any sex-contact while the wife was pregnant or nursing, and blamed the husband who "puts upon her the unbearable burden of being at one and the same time a mistress, an exhausted mother, and a sickly, irritable, hysterical individual. And the husband loves her as his mistress, ignores her as a mother, and hates her for the irritability and hysteria which he himself has produced and produces." His view is taken by many of our noblest men.

While the wife feels that she cannot allow her husband to enter the portals of her body when it has become the sacred temple of a developing life, she should also consider the perpetual strain which nature imposes upon him; and the tender and loving wife will readily find some means of giving him that physical relief which his nature needs.

The exquisite unselfish tenderness which is aroused in a man by the sense of mental and spiritual harmony with a wife who sympathizes with, because she understands his needs is one of the loveliest things in marriage. A wife who knows how to waken this tenderness in a man raises him out of the self-centered slough in which so many men wallow unhappily.

With an ardent man, wholly devoted to his wife and long deprived of her, the time will come when it will be sufficient for him to be near her and caress her for relief to take place without any physical connection, if, as every wife should, she has retained after marriage that dainty modesty which renders the sight of her bosom and of her beauty a privilege and a joy to her husband.

After the birth of the first child the health of the mother and of the baby both demand that there should be no hurried beginning of a second. At least a year should pass before the second little life is allowed to begin its unfolding, so that a minimum of about two years should elapse before the second child is born.

The importance of this, both for the mother and for the child, is generally adequately recognized by medical specialists, and some distinguished gynecologists advocate as much as three or five years between the births of successive children. While in the whole human relation there is no slavery or torture so horrible as coerced, unwilling motherhood, there is no joy and pride greater than that of a woman who is bearing the developing child of a man she adores. It is a serious reflection on our poisoned "civilization" that a pregnant woman should feel shame to appear in the streets. Never will the race reach true health till it is cured of its prurient sickness, and the prospective mother can carry her sacred burden as a priestess in a triumphal procession.

Of the innumerable problems which touch upon the qualities transmitted to the children by their parents, the study of which may be covered by the general term Eugenics, I shall here say nothing: nor shall I deal with the problems of birth and child-rearing. Many writers have considered these subjects, and my purpose in this book is to present aspects of sex-life which have been more or less neglected by others.

While throughout I have omitted the consideration of abnormalities, there is one condition which verges on the abnormal but yet touches the lives of some married people who are individually both normal and healthy, about which a few words need to be said.

It not infrequently happens that two healthy loving people, for no apparent reason, seem unable to have a child.

The old-fashioned view was that the fault lay with the woman, and the reproach of being a barren woman is one which has brought untold anguish to many hearts. It is now beginning to be recognized, however, that in a childless union, the "fault," if fault it be, is as often the man's as the woman's, particularly where the husband is a brain-worker in a city.

Though it is natural that there should not be the same joy for the pair in a child which had not arisen from their own supreme fusion, nevertheless, the man who is generous and broad-minded might find much joy in a child of his wife's, were the obtaining of this child not coupled with the yielding of her body to the embrace of another man, which is so generally and so naturally repugnant to a husband.

Nevertheless now that women have been successfully impregnated by means of injected semen, a new possibility has arisen for any individual pair who are childless and who long for a little one.[1] Where the injection is undertaken by a woman doctor, the husband need have no feeling that his wife has been violated. And while it is not certain that this method would succeed in giving the child she longs for to the woman, yet there are sufficient records in the medical profession of successful artificial insemination for it to offer much hope to a pair who have been denied perfectly normal parenthood either through the husband's actual sterility or the lack of mutual adjustment in their organs, or from an ill-understood lack of chemical affinity.

[I regret having to disillusion the reader on the subject of artificial impregnation. Many attempts at artificial impregnation of the human female have been made, but the successes have been so few and far between, that the method is never likely to acquire a great vogue. For some centuries to come we will have to depend upon the old-fashioned natural method for the perpetuation of the human race. W. J. R.]

The idea that the soul and character of the child can be in any degree influenced by the mental status of the mother during the months of its development as an embryo within her body, is apt to be greeted with pure skepticism – for it is difficult of proof, and repugnant to the male intellect, now accustomed to explain life in terms of chemistry.

Yet all the wisest mothers whom I know vary only in the degree of their belief in this power of the mother. All are agreed in believing that the spiritual and mental condition and environment of the mother does profoundly affect the character and the mental and spiritual powers of the child.

An interesting fact which strengthens the woman's point of view, is quoted (though not in this connection) by Marshall,[2] who says: "It has been found that immunity from disease may be acquired by young animals being suckled by a female which had previously become immune, the antibody to the disease being absorbed in the ingested milk." This particular fact is explainable in terms of chemistry; but it seems to me more than rash for any one in these days of hormones from ductless glands, to deny the possibility of mental states in the mother generating "chemical messengers," which may impress permanent characters in the physiological reactions of the developing child. Ellis says ("Sex and Society"), "The mother is the child's supreme parent, and during the period from conception to birth the hygiene of the future man can only be affected by influences which work through her."

And Alfred Russel Wallace, the great naturalist, thought the transmission of mental influence neither impossible nor even very improbable.[3] I am convinced that it takes place all the time, molding and influencing the hereditary factors.

Hence I suggest that the husband who is deprived of normal fatherhood may yet make the child of his wife's body partly his own, if his thoughts are with her intensely, supportingly and joyously throughout the whole time of the unborn baby's growth. If he reads to her, plays beautiful music or takes her to hear it, and gives her the very best of his thoughts and aspirations, mystical though the conclusion may seem, he does attain an actual measure of fatherhood.

The converse, where the wife is really barren and the husband capable of having children with another woman, is a much more difficult problem. Then the attainment of children by the man is impossible without the collaboration of another woman in a manner not recognized by our laws and customs. Even if this is done, it is clear that to introduce the child of another woman into the home is demanding a much greater self-abnegation from the wife than is demanded from the husband in the situation we have just considered.

Many people whose ideals are very noble are yet strangely incapable of adapting the material acts of life to the real fulfilment of their ideals. Thus there is a section of our community which insists that there should be no restriction whatever of the number of children born to married people. They think any birth control immoral. They take their stand upon the statement that we have no right to destroy potential life. But if they would study a little human or animal physiology they would find that not only every celibate, but also every married man incessantly and inevitably wastes myriads of germs which had the potentiality of fusion with an ovum, and consequently could have produced a child had opportunity been given them. For the supposed sake of one or two of these myriad spermatozoa which must naturally and inevitably die, they encourage the production of babies in rapid succession, which are weakened by their proximity, while they might have been sturdy and healthy, had they been conceived further apart from each other.

Such people, while awake to the claims of the unborn, nay, even of the unconceived, are blind to the claims of the one who should be dearest of all to the husband, and for whose health and happiness he is responsible. A man swayed by such pseudo-religious ignorance will allow his wife to bear and bring forth an infant annually. Save where the woman is exceptional, each child following so rapidly on its predecessor, saps and divides the vital strength which is available for the making of the offspring. This generally lowers the vitality of each succeeding child, and surely even if slowly, may murder the woman who bears them.

Of course, the effects of this strain upon the woman vary greatly according to her original health and vitality, the conditions of her surroundings and the intensity of the family's struggle for food. A half-starved mother trying to bring up children in the foul air of city slums, loses, as a rule, far more of her family than a comfortable and well-fed woman in the country. Nevertheless, conditions are not everything; under the best conditions, the chances of death of the later children of a large family, which comes rapidly, are far greater than for the earlier children.

Dr. Ploetz found that while the death rate of first born infants is about 220 per thousand, the death rate of the seventh born is about 330, and of the twelfth born is 597 per thousand. So that when "nature" has its way, and twelve children come to sap a woman's vitality, so little strength has she that nearly 60 per cent. of these later ones die. What a waste of vitality! What a hideous orgy of agony for the mothers to produce in anguish death-doomed, suffering infants!

Forel ("The Sexual Question") says: "It seems almost incredible that in some countries medical men who are not ashamed to throw young men into the arms of prostitution, blush when mention is made of anti-conceptional methods. This false modesty, created by custom and prejudice, waxes indignant at innocent things while it encourages the greatest infamies."

It is important to observe that Holland, the country which takes most care that children shall be well and voluntarily conceived, has increased its survival-rate, and has thereby not diminished but increased its population, and has the lowest infant mortality in Europe. While in America, where the outrageous "Comstock Laws" confuse wise scientific prevention with illegal abortion and label them both as "obscene," thus preventing people from obtaining decent hygienic knowledge, horrible and criminal abortion is more frequent than in any other country.

It should be realized that all the proper, medical methods of preventing undesired pregnancy consists, not in destroying an already growing embryo, but in preventing the male semen from reaching the unfertilized egg cell. This may be done either by shutting the semen away from the opening of the womb, or by securing the death of all (instead of the natural death of all but one) of the two or three hundred million spermatozoa which enter the woman. Even when a child is allowed to grow in its mother, all these hundreds of millions of spermatozoa are inevitably and naturally destroyed every time the man has an emission; and to add one more to these millions sacrificed by nature is surely no crime! To render inert the ejaculated spermatozoa which would otherwise die and decompose naturally, is a simple matter, now familiar to every intelligent physician and layman. The knowledge is easily obtainable.

To those who protest that we have no right to interfere with the course of nature, one must point out that the whole of civilization, everything which separates man from animals, is an interference with what such people commonly call "nature."

Nothing in the cosmos can be against nature for it all forms part of the great processes of the universe.

Actions differ, however, in their relative positions in the scale of things. Only those actions are worthy which lead the race onwards to a higher and fuller completion and the perfecting of its powers, which steer the race into the main current of that stream of life and vitality which courses through us and impels us forward.

It is a sacred duty of all who dare to hand on the awe-inspiring gift of life, to hand it on in a vessel as fit and perfect as they can fashion, so that the body may be the strongest and most beautiful instrument possible in the service of the soul they summon to play its part in the mystery of material being.

Footnotes

1. This was done by the famous Dr. Hunter at the end of the eighteenth century, and since then various doctors have employed this method. An account of some cases is given by Heape in the Proceedings of the Royal Society, 1897; see also Marshall's text book of "Physiology of Reproduction," 1910.

2. "The Psychology of Reproduction," 1910, p. 566.

3. "Nature," 1893, August 24, pp. 389 and 390.

Society

"Love is fed not by what it takes, but by what it gives, and that excellent dual love of man and wife must be fed also by the love they give to others."

–Edward Carpenter

MAN, even the commonplace modern man, is romantic. He craves consciously or unconsciously for the freedom, the beauty, and the adventure which his forefathers found in their virgin forests. This craving, transmuted, changed out of recognition by civilized life and modern conditions, is yet a factor not to be ignored in the relationship of the sexes.

The "bonds of matrimony," so often referred to with ribald laughter, touch, and perhaps secretly gall, even the most romantic and devoted husband. If to the sincere and friendly question: "What is most difficult in married life for the man?" one gets the sincere answer – that answer would be summed up in the words: "perpetual propinquity."

Of this, the wife, particularly if she be really in love, is seldom fully aware. If her husband is her true lover, his tenderness and real devotion will give him the wit to conceal it. But though by concealment he may preserve the unruffled surface of their happiness, yet the longing to be roving is not completely extinguished. In the true lover this unspoken and unconscious longing is perhaps less a desire to set out upon a fresh journey, than a longing to experience again the exquisite joy of the return; to re-live the magic charm of the approach to the spot in which the loved one is living her life, into the sacred separateness of which the lover breaks, and, like the Prince by his kiss, to stir her to fresh activity.

As will be realized by those who have understood the preceding chapters, each coming together of man and wife, even if they have been mated for many years, should be a fresh adventure; each winning should necessitate a fresh wooing.

Yet what a man often finds so hard is to come to that wooing with full ardor and with that complete sense of romance which alone can render it utterly delightful, if the woman he is to woo has been in a too uninterrupted and prosaic relation with him in the meantime.

Most men, of course, have their businesses apart from their homes, but in the home lives of the great mass of middle-class people, the Victorian tradition still too largely preponderates, and the mated pair bore each other to death during the daily routine.

To a very thoughtful couple of my acquaintance, the sense of romantic joy in one another was so precious that they endeavored to perpetuate it by living in different houses.

Such a measure, however, is not likely to suit many people, particularly where there are children. Yet even without bodily separation (which must always entail expense) or any measure of freedom not at every one's command, much can be done to retain that sense of spiritual freedom in which alone the full joy of loving union can be experienced.

But even intellectual and spiritual freedom is often rendered impossible in present-day marriage.

The beautiful desire for ideal unity which is so strong in most hearts is perhaps the original cause of one of the most deadening features in many marriages. In the endeavor to attain the ideal unity, one partner consciously or unconsciously imposes his or her will and opinions first upon the other partner, and then upon the children as they grow up.

The typical self-opinionated male which this course develops, while a subject for laughter in plays and novels, a laughter which hastens his extermination, is yet by no means extinct. In his less exaggerated form such a man may often be an idealist, but he is essentially an idealist of narrow vision. The peace, the unity for which he craves is superficially attained; but it takes acuter eyes than his to see that it is attained, not by harmonious intermingling, but by super-position and destruction.

I have known a romantic man of this type, apparently unaware that he was encroaching upon his wife's personality, who yet endeavored not only to choose her books and her friends for her, but "prohibited" her from buying the daily newspaper to which she had been accustomed for years before her marriage, saying that one newspaper was enough for them both, and blandly ignoring the fact that he took it with him out of the house before she had an opportunity of reading it. This man posed to himself more successfully than to others, not only as a romantic man, but as a model husband; and he reproached his wife for jeopardizing their perfect unity whenever she accepted an invitation in which he was not included.

On the other hand, in homes where the avowed desire is for the modern freedom of intellectual life for both partners, there is very frequently a bickering, a sense of disharmony and unrest that dispels the peace and the air of restful security which is an essential feature of a true home.

It is one of the most difficult things in the world for two people of different opinions to retain their own opinions without each endeavoring to convert or coerce the other, and at the same time to feel the same tender trust in the judgment of the other that each would have felt had they agreed.

It takes a generous and beautiful heart to see beauty and dignity in the attitude of a mate who is looking at the other side of a vital question.

But the very fact that it does take a beautiful and generous heart to do this thing proves it well worth the doing.

If the easier way is chosen and the two mutually conceal their views when they differ, or the stronger partner coerces the weaker into hiding those traits which give personality to an individual, the result is an impoverishing of both, and through that very fact, an impoverishment, a lowering of the love which both sought to serve.

In marriage each one dreams that he will find the Understander – the one from whom he may set out into the world in search of treasures of knowledge and experience, and before whom the spoils may be exhibited without thought of rivalry, and with the certainty of glad apprisal. Treasures, dear to our own hearts but of no value to others, should here find appreciation, and here the tender super-sensitive germ of an idea may be watered and tended till its ripe beauty is ready to burst upon the world.

As marriage is at present, such tenderness and such stimulating appreciation is much more likely to come from the woman to the man and his work than from the man to the woman. For too long have men been accustomed to look upon woman's views, and in particular on her intellectual opinions, as being something demanding at the most a bland humoring beneath the kindest of smiles.

Even from the noblest man, the woman of sensitive personality to-day feels an undercurrent as of surprised congratulation when she has anything to say worth his serious attention outside that department of life supposed to belong to her "sphere." Thus man robs his wedded self of a greatness which the dual unity might reach.

But in marriage the mutual freedom and respect for opinions, vitally important though they be, are not sufficient for the full development of character. Life demands ever widening interests. Owing partly to the differentiation of many types of individuals due to the specialization of civilization, and partly to the transmutation of his old vagrant instinct, man increasingly desires to touch and to realize the lives of his fellows. In the lives of others our hearts and understandings may find perpetual adventures into the new and strange.

Individual human beings, even the noblest and most complex yet evolved, have but a share of the innumerable faculties of the race. Hence even in a supremely happy marriage, which touches, as does the mystic in his raptures, a realization of the whole universe, there cannot lie the whole of life's experience. Outside the actual lives of the pair there must always be many types of thought and many potentialities which can be realized only in the lives of other people.

In the complete human relation friends of all grades are needed, as well as a mate. Marriage, however, in its present form is too often made to curtail the enjoyment of intimate friendships. The reason for this is partly the social etiquette, which, though discarded in the highest levels of society, still lingers in many circles, of inviting the husband and the wife together upon all social occasions. It is true that they are separated at the dinner table, but they are always within the possibility of earshot of each other, which very often deadens their potentialities for being entertaining. The mere fact of being overheard repeating something one may have already said elsewhere is sufficient to prevent some people from telling their best stories, or from expressing their real views upon important matters.

And, a still more serious barrier to joy, so primitive, so little evolved are we even yet, there is in most human beings a strong streak of sex-jealousy. For either mate to be allowed to go out uncriticized into the world, is to demand, if not more than the other is willing to give, at least a measure of trust which by its rarity appears now-a-days as something conspicuously fine.

Jealousy, which is one of the most frequent shadows cast by the light of love, is very apt to sow a distrust in one which makes a normal life for the other partner impossible.

It is hard to say in which sex the feeling is more strongly developed. It takes special forms under different circumstances, and if a nature is predisposed towards it, it is one of the most difficult characteristics to eradicate.

Custom, and generations of traditions, seem to have imprinted on our race the false idea that marital fidelity is to be strengthened by coercive bonds. We are slowly growing out of this, and now-a-days in most books giving advice to young wives there is a section telling them that a man should be allowed his men friends after marriage.

But this is not enough. There should be complete and unquestioning trust on both sides. The man and the woman should each be free to go unchallenged even in thought, on solitary excursions, or on visits, week-ends or walking tours, without the possibility of a breath of jealousy or suspicion springing up in the heart of the other.

It is true that many natures are not yet ready for such trust, and might abuse such freedom. But the baser natures will always find a method of gratifying their desires, and are not likely to err more in trusted freedom than they would inevitably have done through secret intrigues if held in jealous bondage.

And it is only in the fresh unsullied air of such freedom that the fullest and most perfect love can develop. In the marriage relation it is supremely true that only by loosening the bonds can one bind two hearts indissolubly together.

When they are sometimes physically apart married lovers attain the closest spiritual union. For with sensitive spirits – and they are the only ones who know the highest pinnacles of love – periods of separation and solitude can be revivifying and re-creative.

So great is the human soul that some of its beauty is hidden by nearness: it needs distance between it and the beholder to be perceived in its true perspective.

To the realization of the beauty and the enjoyment of solitude, woman in general tends to be less open than man. This, perhaps, is due to the innumerable generations during which the claims of her children and of domestic life have robbed her of nature's healing gift.

Although it is merely incidental to the drama, yet to me the most poignant thing in Synge's beautiful play Deirdré is that she could feel inevitable tragedy when the first thought of something apart from herself crosses her lover's mind. Deirdré and her lover had been together for seven years in an unbroken and idyllic intimacy, and she feels that all is finished, and that her doom, the knell of their joy, had struck, when for the first time she perceived in him a half-formed thought of an occupation apart from her.

This ancient weakness of our sex must be conquered, and is being conquered by the modern woman.

While modern marriage is tending to give ever more and more freedom to each of the partners, there is at the same time a unity of work and interest growing up which brings them together on a higher plane than the purely domestic one which was so confining to the women and so dull to the men. Every year one sees a widening of the independence and the range of the pursuits of women; but still, far too often, marriage puts an end to woman's intellectual life. Marriage can never reach its full stature until women possess as much intellectual freedom and freedom of opportunity within it as do their partners.

That at present the majority of women neither desire freedom for creative work, nor would know how to use it, is only a sign that we are still living in the shadow of the coercive and dwarfing influences of the past.

In an interesting article on woman's intellectual work, W. J. Thomas ("Sex and Society") says: "The American woman, with the enjoyment of greater liberty has made an approach toward the standards of professional scholarship, and some individuals stand at the very top in their university studies and examinations. The trouble with these cases is that they are either swept away and engulfed by the modern system of marriage, or find themselves excluded in some intangible way from association with men in the fullest sense, and no career is open to their talents."

He sees clearly that this is but a passing phase in the development of our society, and he advocates a wider scope for the play of married women's powers. "The practice of an occupational activity of her own choosing, and a generous attitude towards this on the part of the man, would contribute to relieve the strain and make marriage more frequently successful."

When woman naturally develops the powers latent within her, man will find at his side not only a mate, free and strong, but a desirable friend and an intellectual comrade.

The desire for freedom, both for physical and mental exploration and for experiences outside the sacred enclosure of the home, may at first sight appear to be conflicting and entirely incompatible with the ideal of closer and more perfect unity between the married pair. But this conflict is only apparent, though it is true that most writers have failed to realize this. Consequently, in some sections of the writing and teaching of the "advanced" schools, there are claims only for increased freedom – a freedom to wander at will – a freedom in which the wanderer does not return to his fixed center.

On the other hand there are those who realize principally the beauty of married unity, and, concentrating on the demand for the unity and extremest chastity on the part of the married pair, are very apt to ignore the enriching flow of a wide life's experiences. They try to dam up the fertilizing tide of life, and thus, though they are unconscious of what they are doing, they tend to reduce the richness and beauty of marriage.

It is for the young people of the new generation to realize that the two currents of longing which spring up within them – the longing for a full life-experience and the longing for a close union with a life-long mate – are not incompatible, but are actually both essential parts of the more perfect and fuller beauty of the future that already seeks to find its expression in their lives.

Ellen Key ("Love and Marriage") seems to fear the widening of the married woman's life, and she writes as though the aspiration to do professional and intellectual work of a high order must dwarf and sterilize the mother in the married woman.

She writes of a more northerly people, the Scandinavians, and it may be true of her country-women; I do not know. But it is not essentially and universally true. I am writing of the English-speaking races of to-day, and though we also have among us that dwarfed and sterilized type of woman, she forms in our community a dwindling minority. The majority of our best women enter marriage and motherhood, or else long for a marriage more beautiful than the warped mockery of it that is offered them.

As Mrs. Gilman says ("Women and Economics"):

> "In the primal physical functions of maternity the human female cannot show that her supposed specialization to these uses has improved her fulfilment of them, rather the opposite. The more freely the human mother mingles in the natural industries of a human creature, as in the case of the savage woman, the peasant woman, the working woman everywhere who is not overworked, the more rightly she fulfills these functions. The more absolutely the woman is segregated to sex-functions only, cut off from all economic use and made wholly dependent on the sex-relation as means of a livelihood, the more pathological does her motherhood become. The over-development of sex caused by her economic dependence on the male reacts unfavorably on her essential duties. She is too female for the perfect motherhood!"

The majority of our young women, I am convinced, have in them the potentiality of a full and perfected love. So, too, have the majority of our young men. For the best type of young man to-day is tired of polygamy; he has seen enough in his father's and friends' lives of the weariness of the sinister, secret polygamy, that hides itself and rots the race under the protecting cloak of the supposed monogamy of our social system.

But as things are at present in England and in America, the young man who marries, however much he may be in love, is generally too ignorant (as has been indicated in the preceding chapters) to give his wife real physical delight. Then, sooner or later, comes the sequence of disappointments which culminate in the longing for a fresh adventure.

As one young husband said to me: "A decent man can't go on having unions with his wife when she obviously does not enjoy them," and so he is forced to "go elsewhere." "And they call us polygamists! We are not polygamists. But marriage is a rotten failure," was his verdict.

No. They are not polygamists, the finest young men of the present and of the future. Most men to-day are not in their heart of hearts polygamists, in spite of all the outward signs to the contrary; in spite of the fact that so few of them have remained faithful to one woman. But they are ignorant of the sex-laws and traditions, that sex-knowledge which was the heritage of much less civilized tribes, and so they have trampled and crushed out the very thing for the growth of which their hearts are aching.

Hence secretly (for in a marriage that is at least superficially happy the man seldom does this openly) the man begins to crave for another type of society and he "goes elsewhere." Not, it is true, to find, or even in the hope of finding, what he would get from a perfect marriage; but often to satisfy in some measure that yearning for fresh experience, for romance, and for that sense of fusion with another is the romantic experience which, even if it is only a delusion of the senses, is yet one of the most precious things life has to offer.

It is hard, indeed, in many cases it seems impossible, for a good woman to understand what it is that draws her husband from her. Restricted by habit and convention in the exercise of all her faculties, she is unaware of the ever-narrowing range of her interest and her powers of conversation. The home life tends to become that of a fenced pond, instead of a great ocean with innumerable currents. From the restricted and fenced, man's instinct is ever to escape. Man's opportunities for exploration in the cities are few, and the loose woman is one of the most obvious doors of escape into new experiences.

Women feel a so righteous and instinctive horror of prostitution, and, regarding it, they experience an indignation so intense, that they do not seek to understand the man's attitude.

The prostitute, however, sometimes supplies an element which is not purely physical, and which is often lacking in the wife's relation with her husband, an element of charm and mutual gayety in pleasure.

If good women realized this, while they would judge and endeavor to eliminate prostitution no less strenuously, they might be in a better position to begin their efforts to free men from the hold that the social evil has upon them.

It is perhaps impossible to find the beginning of a vicious circle, but the first step out of it must be the realization that one is within it, and the realization of some, at any rate, of its component parts.

Man, through prudery, through the custom of ignoring the woman's side of marriage and considering his own whim as the marriage law, has largely lost the art of stirring a chaste partner to physical love. He therefore deprives her of a glamour, the loss of which he deplores, for he feels a lack not only of romance and beauty, but of something higher which is mystically given as the result of the complete union. He blames his wife's "coldness" instead of his own want of art. Then he seeks elsewhere for the things she could have given him had he known how to win them. And she, knowing that the shrine has been desecrated, is filled with righteous indignation, though generally as blind as he is to the true cause of what has occurred.

Manifold and far-reaching, influencing the whole structure of society not only in this country, but in every country and at every time, have been the influences which have grown up from the root-fallacy in the marriage relation.

Then there is another cause for the dulling of a wife's bright charm. It is indeed a serious matter, as Jean Finot says, "that, under present conditions, the mistress keeps certain liberties which are denied to married women."

The past and its history have been studied by many, and we may leave it. What concerns the present generation of young married people is to-day and the future. The future is full of hope. Already one sees beginning to grow up a new relationship between the units composing society.

In the noblest society love will hold sway. The love of mates will always be the supremest life experience, but it will no longer be an experience exclusive and warped.

The love of friends and children, of comrades and fellow-workers, will but serve to develop every power of the two who are mates. By mingling the greatness of their individual stature they can achieve together something that, had both or either been dwarfed and puny individuals, would have remained for ever unattainable.

The whole trend of the evolution of human society has been toward an increased coherence of all its parts, until at the present time it is already almost possible to say that the community has an actual life on a plane above that of all the individuals composing it: that the community in fact is a superentity. It is through the community of human beings, and not in our individual lives, that we reach an ultimate permanence upon this globe.

When our relation to the community is fully realized, it will be seen that the health, the happiness, and the consequent powers of every individual, concern not only his own life, but also affect the whole community of which he is a member.

The happiness of a perfect marriage, which enhances the joy of the private life, renders one not only capable of adding to the stream of the life-blood of the community in children, but by marriage one is also rendered a fitter and more perfect instrument for one's own particular work, in the tempering and finishing of which society plays a part, and the results of which should be shared by society as a whole.

Thus it is the concern of the whole community that marriage should be as perfect, and hence as joyous, as possible; so that powers which should be set free and created for the purpose of the whole community should not be frittered away in the useless longing and disappointment engendered by ignorance, narrow restrictions, and low ideals.

In the world the happily mated pair should be like a great and beautiful light; a light not hid under a bushel, but one whose beams shine through the lives of all around them.

The Glorious Unfolding

"Let knowledge grow from more to more, but more of reverence in us dwell."

–Tennyson

WE are surrounded in this world by processes and transmutations so amazing that were they not taking place around us hourly they would be scouted as impossible imaginings.

A mind must be dull and essentially lacking in imagination which can learn without interest or amazement for the first time that the air we breathe, apparently so uniform in its invisible unity, is in reality composed of two principal, and several other, gases. The two gases, however, are but mixed as wine may be with water, and each gas by itself is a colorless air, visually like that mixture of the two which we call the atmosphere.

Much greater is the miracle of the composition of water. It is made of only two gases, one of them a component of the air we breathe, and the other similarly invisible and odorless, but far lighter. These two invisible gases, when linked in a proportion proper to their natures, fuse and are no longer ethereal and invisible, but precipitate in a new substance, water.

The waves of the sea with their thundering power, the sparkling tides of the river buoying the ships, are but the transmuted resultant of the union of two invisible gases. And this, in its simplest terms, is a parable of the infinitely complex and amazing transmutations of married love.

Ellis expresses the strange mystery of one of the physical sides of love when he says:

"What has always baffled men in the contemplation of sexual love is the seeming inadequacy of its cause, the immense discrepancy between the necessarily circumscribed regions of mucous membrane which is the final goal of such love and the sea of world-embracing emotions to which it seems the door, so that, as Remy de Gourmont has said, 'the mucous membranes, by an ineffable mystery, enclose in their obscure folds all the riches of the infinite.' It is a mystery before which the thinker and the artist are alike overcome."

To me, however, the recent discoveries of physiology seem to afford a key which may unlock a chamber of the mystery and admit us to one of the halls of the palace of truth. The hormones, the internal secretions of the so-called ductless glands in each individual body pour from one organ and affect another, and thus influence the whole character of the individual's life processes. The visible secretions and the most subtle essences which pass during union between man and woman, affect the lives of each and are essentially vital to each other. As I see them, the man and the woman are each organs, parts, of the other. And in the strictest scientific, as well as in a mystical, sense they together are a single unit, an individual entity. There is a physiological as well as a spiritual truth in the words, "they twain shall be one flesh."

In love it is not only that the yearning of the bonds of affinity to be satisfied is met by the linking with another, but that out of this union there grows a new and unprecedented creation.

In this I am not speaking of the bodily child which springs from the love of its parents, but of the superphysical entity created by the perfect union in love of man and woman. Together, united by the love bonds which hold them, they are a new and wondrous thing surpassing, and different from, the arithmetical sum of them both when separate.

So seldom has the perfection of this new creation been experienced, that we are still far short even of imagining its full potentialities, but that it must have mighty powers we dimly realize.

Youths and maidens stirred by the attraction of love, feel hauntingly and inarticulately that there is before them an immense and beautiful experience: feel as though in union with the beloved there will be added powers of every sort which have no measure in terms of the ordinary unmated life.

These prophetic dreams, if they are not true of each individual life, are yet true of the race as a whole. For in the dreams of youth to-day is a foreshadowing of the reality of the future.

So accustomed have we recently become to accept one aspect of organic evolution, that we tend to see in youth only a recapitulation of our race's history. The well-worn phrase "Ontogeny repeats Phylogeny" has helped to concentrate our attention on the fact that the young in their development, in ourselves as in the animals, go through many phases which resemble the stages through which the whole race must have passed in the course of its evolution.

While this is true, there is another characteristic of youth: It is prophetic!

The dreams of youth, which each young heart expects to see fulfilled in its own life, seem so often to fade unfulfilled. . . . But that is because the wonderful powers of youth are not supplied with the necessary tool – knowledge. And so potentialities, which could have worked miracles are allowed to atrophy and die.

But as humanity orients itself more truly, more and more will the knowledge and experience of the whole race be placed at the disposal of all youth on its entry into life.

Then that glorious upspringing of the racial ideal, which finds its expression in each unspoiled generation of youth, will at last meet with a store of knowledge sufficient for its needs, and will find ready as a tool to its hand the accumulated and sifted wisdom of the race.

Then youth will be spared the blunders and the pain and the unconscious self-destruction that to-day leaves scarcely any one untouched.

In my own life, comparatively short and therefore lacking in experience though it be, I have known both personally and vicariously so much anguish that might have been prevented by timely knowledge. This impels me not to wait till my experience and researches are complete, and my life and vital interest are fading, but to hand on at once those gleanings of wisdom I have already accumulated which may help the race to understand itself. Hence I conclude this little book, for, though incomplete, it contains some of the vital things youth should be told.

In all life activities, house-building, hunting or any other, where intellectual and oral tradition comes in, as it does with the human race, "instinct" tends to die out. Thus the human mother is far less able to manage her baby without instruction than is a cat her kittens; although the human mother at her best has, in comparison with the cat, an infinitude of duties toward, and influences over, her child.

A similar truth holds in relation to marriage. The century-long following of various "civilized" customs has not only deprived our young people of most of the instinctive knowledge they might have possessed, but has given rise to innumerable false and polluting customs.

Though many write on the art of managing children, few have anything to say about the art of marriage, save those who have some dogma, often theological or subversive of natural law, to proclaim.

Any fundamental truth regarding marriage is rendered immeasurably difficult to ascertain because of the immense ranges of variety in human beings, even of the same race, many of which result from the artificial conditions and the unnatural stimuli so prevalent in what we call civilization. To attempt anything like a serious study of marriage in all its varieties would be a monumental work. Those who have even partially undertaken it have tended to become entangled in a maze of abnormalities, so that the needs of the normal, healthy, romantic person have been overlooked.

Each pair, therefore, has tended to repeat the blunders from which it might have been saved, and to stumble blindly in a maze of difficulties which are not the essential heritage of humanity, but are due to the unreasoning folly of our present customs.

I have written this book for those who enter marriage normally and healthily, and with optimism and hope.

If they learn its lessons they may be saved from some of the pitfalls in which thousands have wrecked their happiness, but they must not think that they will thereby easily attain the perfection of marriage. There are myriad subtleties in the adjustment of any two individuals.

Each pair must, using the tenderest and most delicate touches, sound and test each other, learning their way about the intricacies of each other's hearts.

Sometimes, with all the knowledge and the best will in the world, two who have married find that they cannot fuse their lives; of this tragedy I have not here anything to say; but ordinary unhappiness would be less frequent than it is were the tenderness of knowledge applied to the problem of mutual adjustment from the first day of marriage.

All the deepest and highest forces within us impel us to evolve an ever nobler and tenderer form of life long monogamy as our social ideal. While the thoughtful and tender-hearted must seek, with ever greater understanding, to ease and comfort those who miss this joyful natural development, reformers in their zeal for side-issues must not forget the main growth of the stock. The beautiful sense for love in the hearts of the young should be encouraged, and they should have access to the knowledge of how to cultivate it, instead of being diverted by the clamor for "freedom," to destroy it.

Disillusioned middle age is apt to look upon the material side of the marriage relation, to see its solid surface in the cold, dull light of everyday experience; while youth irradiated by the glow of its dreams is unaware how its aërial and celestial phantasies are broken and shattered when unsuspectingly brought up against the hard facts of physical reality.

The transmutation of material facts by celestial phantasies is to some extent within the power of humanity, even the imperfect humanity of to-day.

When knowledge and love go together to the making of each marriage, the joy of that new unit, the Pair, will reach from the physical foundation of its united body to the heavens where its head is crowned with stars.

Notes

ASSUMING now that the two are in the closest mental and spiritual, as well as sensory harmony: in what position should the act be consummated? Men and women, looking into each other's eyes, kissing tenderly on the mouth, with their arms round each other, meet face to face. And that position is symbolic of the coming together of the two who meet gladly. It is usual in civilized societies for the man to lie above the woman as she reclines on her back. Indeed a curious idea seems to exist that it is "immoral" or "humiliating" for the man if the position is reversed. Yet Ovid recommends it to little women, and where the woman is muscularly delicate and easily crushed there is no doubt that it is a position much more likely to give her pleasure. To make it quite satisfactory to the man, the woman must be tender and supple and skilled in the charm and movements of love-play. When this is so there may be an exquisite grace in the event, as though there had entered into it the poetry and beauty of the picture of the sleeping Endymion over whom the floating goddess Diana stooped.

It seems incredible that to-day educated men should be found who – apparently on theological grounds – refuse to countenance this position. Yet one wife told me that she was crushed and nearly suffocated by her husband so that it took her hours to recover after each union, but that "on principle" he refused to attempt any other position than the one he chose to consider normal.

It is perhaps not generally realized how great are the variations of size, shape, and position of all the sex parts of the body in different individuals, yet they differ more even than the size and character of all the features of the face and hands. It happens therefore that the position which suits most people is unsatisfactory for others. Some, for instance, can only enjoy union when both are lying on their sides. Though medically this is generally considered unfavorable or prohibitive for conception, yet I know women who have had several children and who always used this position. In this matter every couple should find out for themselves which of the many possible positions best suits them both.

I invite letters from those who can confirm, qualify or correct my views from their own experience. To obtain scientific knowledge the largest possible number of individual cases must be studied.

While I believe that the charts I give of the Law of Periodicity of recurrence of desire truly represent the fundamental rhythm of average healthy women, it must be remembered that my theory is new, and every well-authenticated case for or against it will be valuable. All communications will be treated with the strictest confidence.

M. C. Stopes

CPSIA information can be obtained
at www.ICGtesting.com
Printed in the USA
BVHW071022210219
540827BV00001B/208/P